Skyhill Immigrant Stories

Skyhill Immigrant Stories

First Edition 1ˢᵗ Publication First Print on August 6th, 2025

Author Ilryong Moon
Illustrations by Claire Y. Kim
Publisher Gil Su Jang
Distributed in South Korea by Knowledge and Sensibility
Publication Registration 2012-000081

Designed by Hui Young Kim
Edited by Hui Young Kim
Proofread by Jang Hee Han
Marketed by Yoon Gil Kim

Address 1212 Daeryung Post Tower 6th, 298 Beokkot-ro, Geumcheon-gu, Seoul, South Korea
Tel 070-4651-3730~4
Fax 070-4325-7006
E-mail ksbookup@naver.com
Homepage www.knsbookup.com

ISBN 979-11-392-2724-6(03810)
Price 19,000 KRW

Damaged books can be exchanged at the place of purchase
All rights reserved.

Homepage Link

Stories of education, American society, immigrant life, and family shared by the author, a six-term school board member serving in Fairfax County—home to one of the top public school systems in the United States.

Skyhill Immigrant Stories

Written by | Ilryong Moon
Illustrations by | Claire Y. Kim
Translation Assisted by | ChatGPT

Following *Sky Castle School Board Member Stories* (*Hamburger Coke* in English edition), these are the reflections of a retired Harvard-educated attorney who immigrated at age 17 during the difficult 1970s and spent 30 years serving in mainstream American society.

Opening Notes

It has been over 50 years since my family immigrated to the United States during my high school years. That is indeed a long time. Over the decades, I have retired from my profession as an attorney, become a grandfather, and experienced both the challenges and failures of running for elected offices. I now serve my sixth term as a school board member in Fairfax County, Virginia, one of the most outstanding and the largest school districts in the country.

A few years ago, I published my first book titled *Sky Castle School Board Member Stories* in 2020. The following year, an English edition, *Hamburger Coke*, was released—a title suggested by my eldest son. He explained that among the many pieces in the book, the essay titled *"Hamburger Coke"* best captured the overarching theme and essence of my life. These two books compiled about 10 percent of the seven hundred columns I had written or prepared for broadcast in the Korean American media in my area since the late 1990s.

Though my writing skills might not be remarkable, I wanted to share the experiences, information, and reflections from my long journey in mainstream American society, as well as my life as an immigrant. I also hoped to leave a written record of my story for my two American-born sons.

This new book contains another 10 percent of the writings that I had not previously shared. I published it first in Korean earlier this year, and this is the English edition. My hope is to introduce these stories not only to Korean American youth born and raised in the U.S. and their parents but also to American readers—including my granddaughter. I hope that even one essay in this book may resonate with or benefit the reader.

The "Skyhill" in the book's title refers to the name of the street where the apartment complex I first lived in upon immigrating to the U.S. was located. For someone like me, who grew up in the poverty and hardship of Korea in the 1960s and 1970s, that place truly felt like a meeting of the sky and a hill—just as its name implied. As I later learned, my family of five, along with a cousin who joined us a few months later, lived together in that two-bedroom unit in violation of the apartment's management rules. The furniture, mostly from the cheapest stores or secondhand shops, still felt luxurious to us, who had previously lived in a one-room home. That is where my immigrant life began.

Many people helped bring this book to life. I am deeply grateful to The Korea Times Washington D.C., Weekly Washington Media, and radio station AM1310 for publishing my writings and allowing it to be broadcast. Unless otherwise noted, all pieces in this book were originally published in The Korea Times Washington D.C. The dates listed at the beginning of each piece reflect the original newspaper publication or broadcast date. I also resorted to using ChatGPT in editing my drafts and their translations. Unlike the past, I could now rely on it for initial editing and translating. The speed and capability of AI were truly remarkable.

I would also like to thank two people who graciously reviewed the manuscript. Despite not having much time, they willingly agreed without complaint. First, Jayden H. Lee is a recent Langley High School graduate and entering Harvard University this fall. He was in my Sunday school class when he was a ninth grader. I have much admiration for this young man who has so much to offer. Second, Wooyoung Moon is my second son. Some stories in the book are related to him. He is a graduate of Thomas Jefferson High School for Science and Technology in Fairfax County, Virginia. He studied physics, receiving a bachelor's degree from Brown University and a doctoral degree from University of Illinois, Urbana-Champaign.

Most of all, I want to express special thanks to Claire Y. Kim for the illustrations throughout the book, including the cover design. She has just finished her junior year of high school (equivalent to the second year of high school in Korea). Claire is a talented student in many areas—art, music, sports, and academics—and demonstrates exceptional leadership qualities as well. She was selected as my Student Leader for the Fairfax County School Board's Student Leadership Program this year, a distinction granted to only twelve students annually. Despite her busy schedule with studies and extracurriculars, she contributed immensely to this project, and I was deeply moved. I hope that she continues to work diligently and grows into someone who makes meaningful contributions to society and achieves her goals.

To close this opening notes, I share below an essay I wrote last year, reflecting on 50 years as an immigrant and approaching retirement from my 40-year legal career.

Looking Back on Half a Century
August 23, 2024

By the end of this month, it will have been half a century since I immigrated to the United States. It feels a bit surreal that the word "century," which I hear in history class, now applies to my own life. I cannot help but think, "Indeed, I have lived in America for a long time."

I arrived in the U.S. in late August 1974, as a 17-year-old high school student. I came with my mother and two younger sisters. My father had come a year earlier and settled in Alexandria, Virginia, where we were finally reunited as a family.

At that time, there was no Incheon Airport in Korea, so we departed from Gimpo Airport. Except for my father, it was the first time that any of us had ever been on an airplane. The Korean Air had not yet begun service to the east coast of the U.S., so we had to take a now-defunct Northwest Airlines flight. To board the plane, we had to walk out onto the tarmac and climb a stair ramp. Inside the terminal, there was a special farewell area where family members and friends could wave goodbye. It was common to see tearful farewells to loved ones departing for distant countries.

Though the memory is now faint, I believe our flight first stopped in Tokyo. From there, we continued on the same airline to the U.S., to Chicago per my recollection. That is where we cleared immigration and collected our luggage.

I was not just responsible for my own family—we also had to help another family from Daegu City. We met them for the first time at Gimpo Airport: the young wife and two small children of a man who had shared a room with my father in the U.S. for several months. Although I could barely speak more than a few words of English, it was up to me to lead both families—six people in total—through an unfamiliar airport and find our connecting flight to Washington Dulles Airport.

It was far from easy for someone as inexperienced and unprepared as I was. I could not even ask for directions and tried to navigate by constantly checking my watch, only to realize I was walking in the wrong direction. I noticed my five-year-old youngest sister at the back of our group, struggling to drag a large suitcase, trying not to lose sight of us.

I was later told that there was an announcement calling for us over the airport speakers, but I did not hear it perhaps because I could not understand it anyway. Eventually, airline staff had to search for us. By the time we were found, the connecting flight had already departed. The staff reassured us and led us to a quiet area. That night, only the four members of my family were able to catch a later flight. Thanks to that, I was able to contact my father in Virginia and explain the situation. But the young mother had to spend the night with her two small children at a hotel provided by the airline. It broke my heart to leave her there in tears. That was my immigration "initiation" to the U.S.

Fifty years have passed since then.

The first ten years were focused on education. Although I had already completed my first year of high school in Korea, which was the 10th grade, I had to start again as a 10th grader in the American system. I completed three years of high school, went on to college, and majored in East Asian Studies with a focus on China. I even spent a year in Taiwan studying Chinese. After that, I attended law school for another three years.

The next ten years were devoted to practicing law. I began my legal career in Arlington, Virginia, and moved my office to Annandale in the late 1980s. In 1995, I ran for the school board and have now spent 30 years balancing my legal practice with public service. During that time, my two sons were born and raised in the U.S., and I now have a granddaughter and am expecting a second grandchild in November. I started my life here as a high school student, and now I am a grandfather. Both of my parents have passed away.

Even after 50 years, English remains difficult, and life in America does not always feel easy or comfortable. Yet, I am not thinking about returning to Korea to live there. Even after fifty years, an immigrant's life may still feel incomplete.

These days, I am preparing to retire from my legal work.[1] Though I do not plan to stop working entirely, stepping away from something I have regarded as a lifelong vocation for 40 years naturally fills me with a bit of anxiety.

It almost feels like I am immigrating all over again.

---

1) I stepped away from most of my legal practice at the end of November 2024. I am currently finishing up a few remaining matters for clients from home.

My first meal in the United States in the middle of the night. The photo was probably taken by one of my father's Korean coworkers who lived in the same apartment complex. The clock points to almost 4 a.m. It was a time of hunger, and the plate piled high with white rice stands out vividly.

Table of Contents

Opening Notes — 4

Chapter 1 **Life Journey**

Introduction	18
Old Letters	20
Sorting Through Old Books	24
Visit to Taiwan	28
Kim Yong, Lee Hong-Ryeol, and I	32
Finding an Old Benefactor	36
Clothes Alterations	40
Snowstorm Story	43
Go (Baduk)	47
AlphaGo–Lee Sedol Challenge Match	52
0.3-Second Rule	55
Respect for Rules	59
Greed and Hatred	62
Design Defect	66
Understanding Differences	69
Comedy Club	72
Reflecting on Thanksgiving	76

Chapter 2   Immigration Life

Introduction	82
The Reverend Jae Hoon Park	84
A Seat at the Table	88
Meeting My 40-Year Juniors	91
Teaching Our Roots	94
Senior Citizen Student	99
Ramadan Dinner	103

Chapter 3   Education Stories

Introduction	108
Ladder of Social Mobility	110
College Acceptance Notifications	113
Hail Mary	117
Back-to-School Night	120
Role of Principal	123
New Year's Day's Bows	126
Time I Felt Freest	130
Artificial Intelligence	135
Politics of School Superintendents	139
Anonymous Voting	143
Funny Guy	146
Episode from a Visit to Korea	150
Teacher Recruitment from Korea	154

Chapter 4 American Society

Introduction	160
Culture Shock	162
Parenting	165
Free Rider	168
Presidency	171
Studying Languages	173
Father and Son McElveens	176
Mature Split	180
Buying a Meal	183
Drinking with Meals	187
Mother of the Annandale Rotary Club	191

Chapter 5 Relationship with Father

Introduction	196
Father	198
Father's Counterattack	203
Sending Off Father	207
Words I Never Said to My Father	212
Life	215

Chapter 6 Relationship with Children

Introduction	220
Between Father and Son	222
When Children Make Mistakes	226

Conversation with My Younger Son	230
Ring Story	235
Running on Crutches	238
Feedback from Son	241
What is More Important?	244
Compared to TV	247
Santa's Gift	250
Parent's Growing Pains	253
Conditions for Marriage	256

Chapter 7 Food Stories

Introduction	262
Acorn Jello	264
Popcorn	268
Cold Water	271
Pizza and Bagels	274
Egg Foo Young	277
Ramen	280
Ice Cream	284
Closing Notes	287
Author and Illustrator	290
Illustrator's Notes	291
Author's Other Publications	294

Chapter 1
Life Journey

Introduction

As I live through what is now called the era of longevity, having said farewell to both of my parents, retired from a 40-year legal career, and became a grandfather, I find myself increasingly reflecting on the journey of my life. Though I have lived earnestly, there were many moments for which I had a sense of regret and others that left me with lingering feelings of "what if." When I find myself hoping to make better use of the time I have left, I often turn to the path I have already traveled, which, in its own way, becomes a kind of guide.

The writings in this section by no means encompass my whole life. Nor do they represent my most defining experiences or thoughts. Some related pieces were already included in the book I published several years ago. Yet even those moments I once considered embarrassing or inadequate—whether mine or someone else's—seem easier to accept now. Perhaps that is because I must be hoping that others will be generous with my shortcomings.

Our society is made up of people with different standards of judgment, backgrounds, and personalities. So, conflicts are inevitable. But whether we are facing such conflicts or simply walking along our individual life paths, how wonderful it would be if we could show more consideration and kindness to one another.

These days, I find myself gradually losing long-time friends and acquaintances. At times, I am even asked to deliver words of remembrance for them. And I sometimes wonder: when I am gone, what will those who know me say about my life journey?

Old Letters

August 21, 2020

Since I immigrated to the United States after completing my first year of high school, I feel closer to my middle school friends than to my high school classmates in Korea. The middle school I attended had just opened its doors, and I was only the second graduating class. That sense of being part of a new school created a special bond among the classmates.

When I was first randomly assigned to the school, I did not even know where it was—I had to ask around. It was located on a hillside in Siheung-dong, Yeongdeungpo-gu, Seoul. To add to the unfamiliarity, it was a coeducational school, which was still rare at the time.

On the day of the entrance ceremony, the school building looked humble. There were not even enough classrooms for the next incoming class, so construction went on throughout my first year. The schoolyard had been carved out of a rocky hill and had hardly any trees. Every Monday and Saturday morning after assembly, all the students would scatter across the schoolyard to pick up stones—that was our routine.

Whenever it rained, mud from the slopes would wash down and make a mess of the school grounds. To prevent this, we planted trees not only on Arbor Day but even during our career technical classes starting in the second grade. Although we understood that planting trees was a good thing, it felt unfair—even as children—to be doing unpaid labor while also paying tuition.

Class placement was based on academic performance. In third grade, students ranked first to thirtieth were placed in the same class as those ranked at the bottom, from first to thirtieth from the bottom. However, for core subjects like Korean, English, math, and science, classes were reorganized by rank, with the top sixty students grouped together. Non-academic subjects like art, music, and physical education were conducted in our originally assigned homerooms. Spending three years together this way naturally brought us middle school classmates very close. That is why, whenever I visit Korea, I always meet my middle school friends first.

Two years ago, I decided to give those friends a special gift. Before leaving the U.S. for a visit, I received a list of friends who would be coming to see me. I then looked for the old letters they had sent me when I first moved to America. Fortunately, I had kept most of them.

I made photocopies of each letter, placed them in individual envelopes, and handed them out. My friends were surprised. They never imagined that I would still have the letters they had written to me in the 1970s, during their high school and college years, more than 40 years ago. They stared at the letters for a long time, as if rediscovering their former selves through the handwriting of the past. Reading those old messages, they remembered what they had once thought and worried about during those years.

I still have those letters. I do not know exactly why I kept them. I had saved nearly all the letters I received during the ten years after arriving in the U.S. in the mid-1970s, though there have not been many after that. I might have handwritten letters until the mid-1980s and gradually have done so less and less after that.

Even now, I sometimes take a few out and read them. Within those letters lies the version of me from back then. Each letter is a response to something I wrote, and when you consider what I must have written in return, it is clear that my thoughts are reflected in them, too. Some contain religious reflections, others are filled with my friends' worries. Some are a bit embarrassing, and others are deeply moving.

Lately, I have been thinking about reducing the clutter in my home. But I do not think I can bring myself to part with these letters. They are pieces of my life and traces of time I have lived through.

I have thought about scanning and storing them on my computer, but nothing can replace the feeling of pulling them out of an envelope and flipping through the pages with my own fingers.

And now I think—moving forward, I should occasionally write handwritten letters again, especially to the people I love.

Letters and postcards from my middle school friends, my homeroom teacher from 9th grade, and a church friend from college. You can see the address of the Skyhill Road apartment where I first lived in the U.S., as well as the address of the house we moved to later.

Sorting Through Old Books

August 20, 2021

I have been living in the same house for 32 years now. It is a modest home, the second one we purchased within a few years of getting married. For many years, I have thought about moving to a smaller place, but I have not actually followed through.

One of the reasons is that when our two grown children return home for holidays, I think it might bring them comfort to find the house they grew up in still the same. My older child moved here before turning two, and the younger one was born and raised in this very home. But in truth, the bigger reason may be that I simply do not feel up to the task of sorting through everything I have accumulated over the years.

I am not someone who throws things away easily.

I still keep handwritten letters I received starting in 1974, when I immigrated as a high school student. I even have the inaugural issue of a church youth magazine published in Korea. I have kept the program from the graduation worship service held for Korean college graduates in the Boston area.

Among the things I find hardest to part with are books. Many I have already read, but there are plenty I have shelved with the thought, "I will read that someday." Some of my favorite books from high school I even wrapped in white protective covers.

Still, whether soon or later, I will need to pare down if I am ever going to move. Books cannot be an exception. So recently, I made a rather big decision: I chose to let go of my full set of Encyclopedia Britannica and a collection of old Baduk (Go) magazines.

It may be hard to believe that anyone still owns an encyclopedia set these days. Today, almost any information can be found online. But back in the 1970s and 1980s, when I first immigrated, Britannica was considered an essential item in the Korean American community.

First-generation immigrant parents did not have much money, but having come to America for their children's future, they were deeply committed to education. So, it was hard to say no when a salesperson emphasized how necessary the encyclopedias were.

Among Korean parents, it was common to hear, "We bought a set for our kids." Many scraped together the money, despite tight budgets, to invest in a set. My parents were no different. Working long hours at multiple jobs—cleaning hotels, schools, and homes—they eventually bought a 30-volume set.

Honestly, though, we did not use the encyclopedias much. We just did not have that much need for them. Yet I kept the set on my bookshelf for nearly 40 years. Now, I have finally decided to let it go.

I will keep just one photo for memory's sake—and send that photo to my children, with a message:

"It was your grandparents' sacrifice and love that made me who I am, and because of that, you exist today."

As for the Baduk magazines, I have collected about one hundred over the years.

When I was a college freshman, the late Cho Nam-Chul, the most respected figure in the Korean Baduk world at the time, visited Boston to promote the game. I was asked to serve as his interpreter, probably because people knew I was a fan of Baduk. That connection led the Korean Baduk Association to send me magazines for many years.

Today, we can easily find Baduk news and game records online, so the need for printed magazines has faded. But back then, they were a major way to spread awareness of the game. Now, I have decided to keep just one issue and take a photo of the rest before letting them go.

There are still many other things I need to sort through. It is not easy when each item holds memories. But just because something is no longer visible does not mean the memory vanishes from the heart. To avoid being stuck in the past, I need to carry those memories forward—in my heart, in writing, and in photographs—and keep moving ahead.

Baduk magazines that Master Cho Nam-Chul sent me over the years through the Korea Baduk Association.

The Encyclopaedia Britannica.

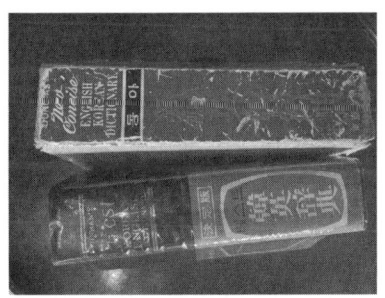

Dictionaries I brought with me from Korea when I immigrated to the United States.

Visit to Taiwan

December 1, 2023

When I think back on the most peaceful period of my life, I often return to the year I spent in Taiwan during college, having taken a leave of absence after immigrating to the United States a few years earlier and enrolling in university. After completing my junior year in college, I felt the need to study Chinese more seriously. I even considered the future as a diplomat. But in 1979, diplomatic relations between the United States and China had only just been restored, and students like me were not yet permitted to study in mainland China. That left only two options for learning Chinese: Hong Kong or Taiwan. I chose Taiwan. It was a larger country than Hong Kong, and unlike Hong Kong, English was not a commonly used language—so I would be less tempted to rely on it.

I did not want the pressure of earning academic credit, so instead of joining a study abroad program offered through my university (which would have allowed me to earn credits through a partner school), I took a leave of absence and chose to study Chinese in my own way. Since I had already been placed a year and a half behind my original grade level when I immigrated, I was older than most of my classmates anyway, so taking another year off did not feel like a burden. I did not see the need to rush through graduation.

Looking back, I have not experienced that kind of ease and freedom in life again—even now, well into my mid-sixties. That is why, as I raised my children and mentored young people around me, I often encouraged them to seek out similar experiences. I would say, "There is no need to sprint through life like it is a 100-meter dash. Treat it like a marathon—pace yourself." I also emphasized the value of living in an environment completely different from one's own.

Perhaps they listened because each of my children found ways to create those opportunities. My older son took time between jobs to spend several months living in a developing country. My younger son participated in a program during his Ph.D. studies that allowed him to conduct research in Europe for a semester. Experiencing firsthand how others live in different circumstances greatly broadens one's perspective and deepens one's capacity for empathy.

Thinking back on those memories, I recently took a few days to revisit Taiwan. After the November school board elections, I decided to take a short break. This was not my first time back since college, but it had been more than 30 years since my last visit, so I felt excited. The weather in Taiwan, much warmer than in Seoul where I had stopped first, reminded me of my younger days filled with dreams, warming both body and spirit.

I had several meaningful goals for this trip. First, I wanted to meet my son's in-laws, whom I had not been able to greet in person due to the pandemic. Though I had attended the wedding in the U.S., my daughter-in-law's parents could not travel from Taiwan because of government health restrictions. This visit gave me the opportunity to express my gratitude to them for welcoming my son into their family, and we had a meaningful time getting to know each other better.

Another purpose of my trip was to visit the pastor of the church I had attended during my time in Taiwan. He was now nearly 90 years old, and I felt a sense of urgency to see him while I still could. Earlier this year, after losing my own father—who was of a similar age—I came to realize deeply that our elders would not always be with us. I wanted to express my thanks while there was still time. Though now thin and stooped with age, the pastor still actively continued his missionary work, and I was deeply moved by his enduring commitment. I wished him good health and prayed that his ministry would continue for many years to come.[2]

Lastly, I sought out the area where I had lived during my college days. Of course, I could not enter the small apartment where I once stayed, but walking down the familiar alley brought back memories. I even passed the small eatery where I used to buy breakfast—youtiao (fried dough) and shaobing (flatbread) with doujiang (soy milk). I vividly remembered starting my mornings with that simple meal, which cost less than 25 cents at the time.

I do not know if I will have another chance to visit Taiwan, but I am grateful for this trip that allowed me to reconnect with a meaningful period in my life. Reflecting on my younger self and the dreams I once held made this a truly rewarding and memorable journey.

---

2) Missionary Kim Dal-Hoon passed away in February 2025 in Taiwan. He was laid to rest at Manghyang Cemetery in Cheonan, South Korea.

During my 2023 visit to Taiwan, with Pastor Dal-Hoon Kim and other Korean missionaries.

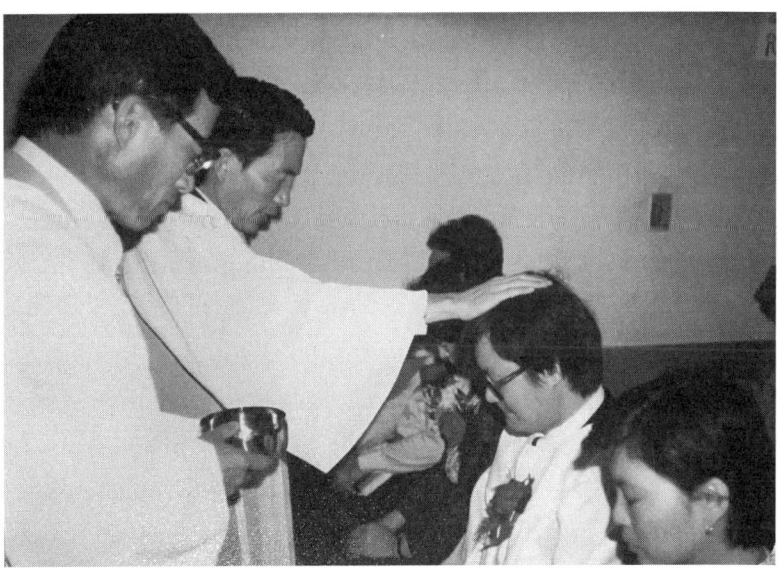

In the spring of 1980, during my time studying in Taiwan, Pastor Dal-Hoon Kim baptizing me at the Taipei Korean Church I was attending.

Kim Yong, Lee Hong-Ryeol, and I

April 5, 2013

I believe it was March of 2009. One day, as I was flipping through a local Korean American community newspaper, I was startled by a large photograph—it looked exactly like me. The nearly closed eyes, the broad forehead, and the distinct facial features—eyes, nose, and mouth—were strikingly similar to mine. When I showed the newspaper to people around me, everyone agreed: the resemblance was uncanny. The person in the photo was Kim Yong (Jim Yong Kim).

The reason his photo had appeared in the paper at the time was that he had just been appointed president of Dartmouth College. He was the first Asian to become president of an Ivy League university in the United States. Born in Seoul in 1959, he immigrated to Iowa with his family at age five. Raised in a well-off family, he earned his undergraduate degree from Brown University and received both his M.D. and Ph.D. in anthropology from Harvard. He later served as chair of the Department of Global Health and Social Medicine at Harvard Medical School and also headed the HIV/AIDS department at the World Health Organization (WHO). He co-founded a medical nonprofit that spearheaded major tuberculosis treatment campaigns. Then, in

March 2012, he was appointed president of the World Bank by President Obama—the first Korean American ever to hold that position.

Meanwhile, Lee Hong-Ryeol is a well-known Korean comedian and TV host, five years older than Kim Yong. He had dreamed of becoming a comedian since middle school, but due to financial hardship, he had to attend a vocational high school instead. Unable to afford college, he worked after graduation but never gave up on his dream of becoming an entertainer. After many failed attempts to break into the industry, he enlisted in the military. Following 33 months of service, he finally debuted in March 1979 through radio and television. Through consistent effort, he eventually rose to become one of the top comedians and hosts in Korea.

Interestingly, Lee Hong-Ryeol also bears a striking resemblance to me. Since he is older, it would be more accurate to say that I resemble him. From his short stature and half-closed eyes to his large face and broad forehead—we looked like mirror images. So, if I resemble Lee Hong-Ryeol, and Kim Yong resembles me, then it follows that Kim Yong and Lee Hong-Ryeol must resemble each other as well. In other words, the three of us, not too far apart in age, look like we could be brothers.

Years ago, the Lee Hong-Ryeol Show was aired on Korean-language TV in the community. It was broadcast once a week, and I would watch it occasionally. I particularly enjoyed a cooking segment called Cham Cham Cham. As the show gained popularity, people around me started saying that I looked like

Lee Hong-Ryeol. At the time, I did not feel great about it—it felt like they were teasing me. Still, I pretended not to mind. I would respond, "It is an honor to hear that. Honestly, I would be lucky to become someone like Lee Hong-Ryeol. It is not easy to become the best in your field like he has. I hope to be similarly recognized in my own profession." I said that because I realized that feeling upset about being told I looked like someone else was no different than denying my own appearance.

However, years later, when people began saying I looked like Kim Yong, I had a completely different emotional response. Unlike with Lee Hong-Ryeol, I felt flattered. I no longer felt the need to justify myself with remarks like, "Kim Yong is such an accomplished person—I should try to be someone worthy of such a comparison."

But this made me reflect on something: while my appearance had not changed, my reaction to the comparison had—depending on who I was being compared to. Was I unconsciously placing different values on people based on their professions or social status? The stark contrast between how I felt being compared to the president of the World Bank versus a comedian suggested there was some implicit bias at play.

In truth, Lee Hong-Ryeol has no reason to be seen as lesser than Kim Yong, especially considering the obstacles he overcame. Despite growing up in a difficult environment, he pursued his dream with unwavering determination and succeeded. Regretting not having gone to college earlier, he enrolled in his mid-thirties and graduated after four years of diligent study. There is much

I can learn from him. And yet, I made the mistake of evaluating people based on their status.

As a school board member who often emphasizes the importance of true character education, I was ashamed to realize I had not fully lived out those values in my own heart.

Finding an Old Benefactor

July 9 & July 23, 2021

Not too long ago, I was suddenly reminded of someone who helped me really long ago—an old benefactor tucked away in my memory.

It was during the summer break after my first year of law school. A friend and I took a road trip to Nova Scotia, Canada. We were driving my old car without air conditioning, but had made sure it was roadworthy before the trip.

Departing from Virginia, we passed through Boston and continued heading north when the car began to malfunction. Even after lifting my foot off the accelerator, the engine would not slow down. I could reduce the speed using the brakes, but the engine's RPM would not drop. Each time we stopped, I had to pop open the hood and manually reset the accelerator lever.

Stop signs and red lights were particularly stressful. I would press down on the brakes with all my strength while my friend would quickly jump out, open the hood, and adjust the lever. We also worried constantly that the engine might suddenly stall. Still, we did not know where to go for repairs in an unfamiliar place. Eventually, we drove all the way to Bar Harbor, Maine, loaded the car onto a ferry, and landed in Yarmouth, Nova Scotia. From there, we drove to Halifax, the capital city, to try to get the car fixed.

But again, we did not know where to start. That is when I thought of reaching out to a fellow Korean—someone who might give us more trustworthy guidance in a foreign land. In the early 1980s, public phone booths were easy to find, and they still had printed phone books inside. I randomly looked up someone with the last name "Kim" and dialed.

Luckily, someone answered. After I explained our situation, the person gave me the name and number of another Korean—also named Kim—who was well known in Halifax as a taekwondo master. I called him, and he picked up right away. He asked where I was, then told me to pull out a map and gave me detailed directions to his taekwondo studio.

That is how I met Master Kim. At the time, he also ran a motel. He offered us a room free of charge and even treated us to dinner at the Japanese restaurant on the first floor of the motel. The next day, we took the car to a repair shop he recommended, toured Halifax, and were able to return home safely.

I think I sent a thank-you card afterward, though I am not entirely sure—it has been too long. What is most unfortunate is that I did not record his full name. He appeared to be in his late thirties or early forties at the time, and I recently felt a strong urge to find him before it is too late. But I did not know where to begin.

I searched online but could not find any information. All I had was the vague memory that he was known as "Master Kim" and ran a taekwondo school in Halifax in the early 1980s. Eventually, I reached out to a longtime taekwondo master in Virginia. He did not know the person either but said he would ask a friend in Halifax.

Through that friend, I received the name "Kim Kwang-Young." But it turned out that he had moved to Ottawa around the mid-1980s.

So, I contacted the Korean Association in Ottawa, but they had no information. They suggested I try the Korean Associations in Toronto and Nova Scotia. I also reached out to Master Lee Tae-Eun in Ottawa, known as the "father of taekwondo in Canada," but I still could not locate him.

Then one day, I received a call from Master Choi Eung-Gil, whom I deeply respect. He had heard I was looking for Master Kim and had reached out to several taekwondo contacts across Canada. To my amazement, he had found him and even spoken to him directly. The name was slightly different from what I remembered—his full name was Master Kim Yang-Kwang.

I sent a text to the number Master Choi had given me, and then nervously called. But Master Kim did not remember me. He had no recollection of helping me. Perhaps that was because he had helped so many people over the years. But instead, he apologized for not having taken better care of me back then, saying he had been juggling multiple businesses at the time.

Even after 40 years, the conversation was warm and easy. I had assumed he was in his late thirties or early forties back then, and our conversation confirmed that he was 12 years older than I, and we were both born in the Year of the Rooster. When I mentioned our shared zodiac sign, he laughed and said, "They say Roosters are smart and hardworking, but end up spending everything they earn." He added that he had worked hard but did not have much left to show for it. His tone was affectionate—like an older brother talking to his younger sibling.

As we chatted, we discovered many unexpected similarities. We had both immigrated the same year and each had two children—he with two daughters, and I with two sons. His eldest daughter and my first younger sister had graduated from the same university, and our second children had attended the same college as well. We laughed together, enjoying the strange but happy coincidences.

He now lives in a part of Canada near Detroit, Michigan. Although the pandemic has closed the border, he said he hopes to visit his daughters in the U.S. once travel restrictions are lifted— and that he would love to meet me when that happens.

I am grateful I had the chance to finally express the gratitude I had clumsily left unspoken as a young student. And through this encounter, I was reminded once again: help that is given without expecting anything in return leaves a lasting and positive impact—even decades later.

None of us can go through life without help from others. We must remember the help we have received—and strive to give back even more. And above all, we must not forget to express our thanks to those who once reached out a hand when we needed it most.

Clothes Alterations

May 27, 2022

About a week ago, I had my photo taken with a Korean woman at an event. She was much taller than I was. Standing side-by-side for the photo seemed a bit awkward for her, and she slightly bent her posture. Over the years, I have grown used to standing next to women taller than I, but she seemed less comfortable with it. It was not until I said, "Let's just stand up straight," that we were finally able to take the picture naturally.

I take after my mother, not my father, and I am short. I also have short arms and legs, which make buying clothes a challenge. As a lawyer, I often wear suits and dress shirts, but finding shirts that fit me right has never been easy.

It is nearly impossible to find dress shirts that fit both my neck and arm length—even in Korea. If I buy a shirt based on my neck size, I almost always have to shorten the sleeves. This often makes the proportions look awkward. That is why, a long time ago, I decided to switch to custom-made shirts from Korea.

Ordering several shirts at once did not cost much more than buying off-the-rack shirts at a U.S. department store and paying for alterations. And since they were custom-made, I could have them tailored not just for my sleeves, but for torso length and fit. Whenever I visited Korea, I had a few made and brought them back. If I could not go in person, I would contact the tailor who had my measurements on file, let them know the fabric and color I wanted, and they would make and send them to me.

But one time, I had a stressful experience with a dress shirt.

It was during my first year of college, over winter break. My parents and I were invited to dinner at the home of a Korean family who had recently immigrated. They had a daughter my age who wanted to go to college and ask me questions.

This brought on a dilemma: what should I wear?

Just three years earlier, we had begun our life as struggling immigrants, and I had few decent clothes. I was barely managing to pay for college at the time. I did have one winter suit, so I decided to wear that.

But the problem was the dress shirt. I did not have one that fit, so I borrowed one from my father. The sleeves were far too long. As a quick fix, I folded the excess and pinned up the sleeves with safety pins.

We arrived for dinner.

As soon as we sat down, the host encouraged me several times to take off my jacket and eat comfortably. I politely declined, but she kept insisting. My mother, sitting next to me, was visibly flustered.

I kept saying, "I am fine, really," and ate my meal with the jacket on.

Sweat ran down my back—not from the hot soup, but from nerves. I do not remember how the dinner ended or how we got home.

There was another similar episode, years later, during a visit to Korea.

I had arranged a lunch with two female friends who used to attend the same church that I did before I immigrated. Before the meal, I stopped by Namdaemun (South Gate) Market to pick up a few casual pants. The prices were so low that even if the pants did not last long, it would not have felt like a waste. But, of course, they needed hemming.

The shopkeeper took my measurements and marked the pants for shortening, then sent me to a nearby alteration shop. But the tailor looked surprised and insisted on measuring me again. She suspected the store had measured me incorrectly.

"Goodness," I thought, "Why doesn't she just shorten them as instructed?"

But even after re-measuring, the results did not change.

Thankfully, the two old church friends, who had known me for over 45 years, were completely unfazed. I was grateful for that.

The Creator made every person different. My height and proportions must also be part of His design. Because of it, I have learned to better understand myself—and to empathize with others in similar situations.

And I have been given the opportunity to write stories like this.

For all of that, I am truly thankful.

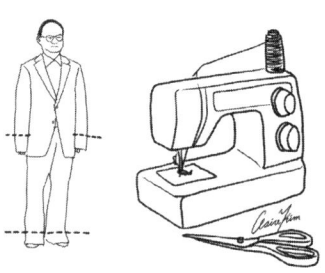

Snowstorm Story

February 19, 2021

Although I have experienced many snowstorms while living in the U.S., none has remained in my memory quite like the Blizzard of 1983. At the time, I was a second-year law student, and with Lunar New Year approaching, I planned to return to my parents' home in Alexandria, Virginia, to keep a promise I had made to some friends. My last class ended at 11 a.m. on Friday, and I figured I would be home in time for late lunch.

A younger female undergraduate student had asked me for a ride. I had given her rides before, and since her house was close to the highway, it would not be out of the way. I agreed without hesitation.

As we left Williamsburg and passed Richmond, snow began to fall. I had not checked the weather forecast—my first mistake. The flakes grew thicker, and by the time we reached Fredericksburg, traffic had come to a complete standstill. At one point, we were stuck in one spot for over two hours. We were hungry, but there was no food in the car and no way to exit the highway to find any.

Not knowing how long we would be trapped, I turned off the engine to conserve fuel. The car quickly grew cold. When it became unbearable, I would restart the engine briefly to warm us up. Snow piled up on the windshield, and the wipers eventually froze, rendering them useless. I had to step out of the car to clear the snow by hand, but as I stepped into the snow, my shoes and socks got soaked and began to freeze. My feet grew so cold that I could not bear going out again. In the end, I had to swallow my pride and ask my younger female passenger to clear the snow instead.

We eventually found a way off the highway and onto local Route 1, but things were not much better there. On uphill roads, cars were barely crawling up one by one, with some sliding back or veering off into ditches. When that happened, drivers at the bottom of the hill would get out to help push them up or pull them out. It was already dark, and dinnertime had long passed. But hunger was the least of our concerns—we were exhausted from the cold and the stress.

I then realized I would not be able to take her all the way home. So, I asked her to call her parents to see if they could meet us halfway. Since this was before smartphones, she had to run to a nearby payphone. When she returned, her face was streaked with tears. Her parents had scolded her for coming home in such weather and told her to find a motel and stay there overnight—they could not come to get her.

That was not an option. We had no money for a motel, and likely no vacancy anyway. Besides, she was a young woman. I reassured her, and we pressed on.

We finally reached her neighborhood. Seeing the snow piled up along the street, I understood why her parents had not been able to drive. My car could not go any farther either, so we parked by the road and walked. The atmosphere in her house was cold—literally and figuratively. I soon found out their second daughter, who had been traveling home from another college [3]with friends, had lost contact. Her parents were understandably on edge. I quietly asked for a bowl of ramen, ate it, and left.

Now I had to get home.

How I did it, I honestly do not remember. When I finally reached my neighborhood, I was too exhausted to continue driving. I left my car parked on the road and walked the rest of the way. I arrived at 12:30 a.m.—thirteen and a half hours after leaving Williamsburg.

Still, I kept my plans with my friends the next day. Few restaurants were open, so we drove all the way into Washington, D.C. to find one. Over drinks, we shared stories of our snowy ordeals. The streets were so empty it was eerie—not a single car in sight.

On the way back to Virginia, on the 14th Street Bridge, the three of us were suddenly overcome by the urgent need to relieve ourselves. With no one else around, we stopped the car in the middle of the bridge. We stood facing the Potomac River, eyes fixed ahead, and... relief. A bold moment possible only in our twenties. I miss that kind of recklessness.

According to Dulles Airport records, snowfall that day measured 22.8 inches.[4]

---

3) Virginia Polytechnic Institute (VPI) located in Blacksburg, Virginia, was much further away.

4) About 60 centimeters.

This photo shows the snow piled up behind our house on February 6, 2010. I wasn't able to take any pictures during the heavy snowfall of 1983—it was a time before smartphones.

Go (Baduk)

May 11, 2012

Last week, diplomatic tensions between the U.S. and China spiked over the case of Chinese blind human rights lawyer Chen Guangcheng. In following the news, I read that Professor Jerome Cohen of NYU Law School played a crucial role in resolving the matter. Chen had reportedly named Cohen as a trusted advisor to American officials. Professor Cohen, it turns out, had previously been involved in the campaign to save former South Korean President Kim Dae-jung and had also assisted Annette Lu, the former vice president of Taiwan.

Reading about Professor Cohen reminded me of a Korean professor who had served as a research scholar at the same law school during my college days. I had heard that he had come to the U.S. seeking refuge from political repression in Korea, and that he, too, was receiving help from Professor Cohen.

This Korean professor had stylish air about him. He wore a hunting cap and tweed jackets with leather elbow patches—like a classic Ivy League professor. He had a commanding presence and smoked a pipe. To me, a college student at the time, he made quite an impression.

He was also an avid Go (baduk) player. Back in Korea, during his time as a university professor, he once reached the semifinals of the professional qualification tournament. Had he won one more game, he could have become a pro. But unlike the other semifinalists, he had no intention of turning pro, so he did not give it his all. That story alone showed how exceptionally skilled he was for an amateur.

At the time, one of the Korean graduate students—who was also a government official—was a strong Go player, and he and the professor often played outside the library. I sometimes watched their games. The professor seemed a bit stronger, but the wins went back and forth. The two of them, forgetting their research and studies, would spend late nights across a Go board rather than books.

Go has a way of stirring up one's pride more than you could imagine. One time, I had the opportunity to play a game with the professor. Though I was far less skilled, he welcomed any opportunity to play. But when it came time to set the handicap, we disagreed. He told me to take four stones, but I stubbornly insisted on only three.

Under normal circumstances, it would have been proper to yield to someone nearly twenty years my senior. But this time, I just could not. I declared, "If not three stones, I will not play," and stood up. I remember another Korean graduate student nearby looking at me with an awkward expression. Still, the professor—so fond of Go—grabbed my arm as I was walking away and said, "All right, let's play with three." He generously overlooked my impudence as a much younger student.

Ironically, years later, when Cho Nam-Chul, the founding father of modern Korean Go, visited Boston to promote the game,

I was asked to interpret for him. There was a teaching game event included in the schedule, and I was offered a chance to play—but for some reason, I politely declined. However, the professor and Master Cho ended up playing.

Even then, there was tension in deciding the handicap. Master Cho said the professor should take three stones, but the professor insisted on two. The master remarked that in Korea, only amateur champions would dare to play him with a two-stone handicap. The professor confidently replied that his skills were at that level.

Master Cho was about twenty years older than the professor, so this time the professor was obstinate. But once again, the elder yielded. He allowed the two-stone game.

The game began with the professor in control from the opening. But as is often the case in Go, the tide turned in the end game. Master Cho ultimately won coming from behind, and the professor looked disappointed. Still, it was not a crushing loss, and it is quite common to lose close games against stronger players in such matchups, especially in the end games.

Even now, I occasionally play Go. But unlike before, I find it harder to focus on reading out the moves. It is too early to blame age, so I comfort myself by saying it is because life has become too busy.

Go players take immense pride in their skills. Yes, they will sometimes deliberately lose a game or pretend it to be nothing even when they win. Yet one poor move—one careless mistake—can ruin an otherwise excellent game. Then, the regret lingers, regardless of age.

Life is not particularly different from a game of Go. We all make occasional missteps. Sometimes, a single move can lead to irreversible consequences. But those mistakes, too, are part of the whole. In Go—and in life.

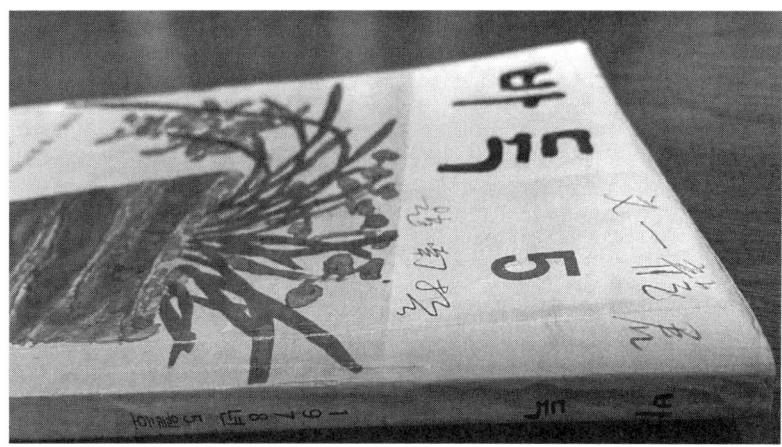

The May 1978 issue of a Baduk (Go) magazine signed and sent to me by Master Cho Nam-Chul. I can see my name in it as well.

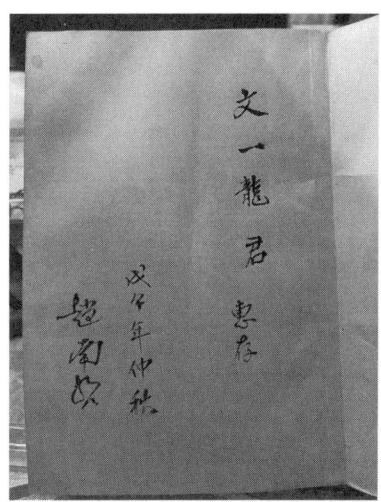

Master Cho Nam-Chul's book Living for Baduk (바둑에 살다)

Inside Living for Baduk, Master Cho Nam-Chul's autograph dedicated to me by name.

AlphaGo–Lee Sedol Challenge Match

March 18, 2016

Over the past week, I hardly slept for five nights in a row. Not even during college or law school exam weeks did I stay up this much. It was all because of the five-game challenge match between Google DeepMind's AlphaGo and 9-dan professional Lee Sedol.

This match drew widespread attention not only in Korea but also within the Korean American community in the U.S. Watching the live broadcasts on YouTube, countless thoughts crossed my mind.

First, staying up into the early morning hours—games started at 11 p.m. or midnight Eastern Time and lasted four to five hours—made me realize how much affection I still held for the game of Go. These days, I rarely play, perhaps just a game or two with a friend now and then. I did not think I would be the type to lose sleep over watching matches. But I did. And I battled fatigue all week as a result.

If judged by wins and losses, the victory went to artificial intelligence. But if we focus on Go itself, I dare say it was a victory for humanity.

Go is not merely a game to determine a winner or loser.

It is a creation of humankind, and its value lies not solely in competition. Of course, everyone plays to win, and we all strive to improve. AI can certainly help us in that regard. But Go carries meanings beyond victory or defeat.

In this match, the duel between human and AI was undoubtedly compelling. Still, rather than simply measuring superiority in intelligence, perhaps the real value lay in exploring the boundaries of both man and machine.

The pressure and psychological toll that only humans experience may be seen as a weakness. Yet it is precisely this vulnerability that gives rise to what we call "humanity," and for that, we can be grateful.

In contrast, when a machine makes what looks like a mistake, we call it a malfunction—something to be overcome for improved performance. While we forgive human errors and limitations, we see the same in machines as flaws. And if a machine could feel emotion like a human, perhaps it would suffer even greater pressure than we do.

Though I am no expert, I was amazed by some of the moves I witnessed. Thanks to the excellent commentary, I was able to understand the meaning of many of them. But some of AlphaGo's moves did not just strike me as unconventional—they felt almost rude in a human sense. In a game between two people, even if one held a clear advantage, some of those moves might never have been played out of respect.

Google reportedly achieved immense marketing success through this challenge. Some estimate its value in billions of dollars. In Korea, public interest in Go surged dramatically.

More students began learning the game, and Go equipment sales soared. Even people who had never taken an interest in Go were suddenly paying attention. This is heartening news for the Go community.

I have long wished that more students in Fairfax County had access to Go. Currently, it is only offered as a special activity at a few schools. But Go is not just a game confined to East Asia. It has the potential to spread globally. I see it as a cultural treasure that Korean Americans can proudly share with the broader American society.

That is why I brought a Go board to last week's regular School Board meeting. I introduced the game and the recent challenge match to my fellow board members and senior school officials. A few colleagues later told me they wanted to learn the game. I plan to send them some YouTube videos explaining the basic rules.

This weekend, I hope to replay and study the records of all five games. I am already excited.

And there is something I would like to say directly to Lee Sedol 9-dan:

"You did an outstanding job. And congratulations. The thrill of your win in Game 4—and the bittersweet ending in Game 5—still linger vividly in my heart."

0.3-Second Rule

February 7, 2014

I recently learned about something called the "0.3-second rule" in basketball. In high school games, if there are 0.3 seconds or less remaining on the clock, a player can only score with a quick tip-in off an inbound pass or rebound. The rule recognizes that 0.3 seconds is not enough time to catch the ball and make a controlled shot.

This rule became the center of controversy in a recent high school basketball game held in Fairfax County, Virginia. The score was 78 to 77, and the trailing team had one final chance to win. With just 0.2 seconds remaining, the coach of the leading team called a timeout and asked the referee to confirm the 0.3-second rule. "All they can do now is tip the ball, right?" he asked. The referee nodded in agreement.

Based on that confirmation, the coach told his players to guard only under the basket. There was no need to cover players farther out, so he placed his tallest defenders near the rim. The offensive coach, also aware of the rule, instructed his players to lob the ball toward someone under the basket for a tip-in.

When play resumed, the inbounding player panicked after seeing the paint heavily guarded and instead passed the ball to a teammate in the corner. The player caught the ball and launched a jump shot.

Recalling the 0.3-second rule, the defending coach raised his hand to signal that the shot was invalid. But to everyone's surprise, the ball sailed through the hoop, and the referee counted the basket—three points. The scoreboard changed to 80–78.

The defending coach immediately protested and remained on the court, knowing that formal game-related protests had to be made at the game site. However, as soon as the match ended, all four referees quickly left the gym and never returned.

The losing team later filed an official protest with the league after confirming the 0.3-second rule. Their argument was that referees could not disregard a rule they themselves had acknowledged during the game. But the league responded differently. While they admitted the referees had made a mistake, they said the outcome could not be overturned. According to league policy, correcting referee errors is allowed only in limited situations—such as ending a game prematurely or wrongly declaring a tie. If every mistake could alter a game's result, they argued, the number of protests would skyrocket, and chaos would follow.

So, what happens when rules exist, but referees do not enforce them? What is the value of a rule that can be ignored, even when everyone acknowledges it was violated? The league stood firm: overturning the result would itself violate another rule. Since the referees' mistake was not intentional, the score would stand. But if the league had reversed the outcome, they said that would have constituted a willful violation of policy.

In the end, the presence or absence of intent became the key factor in determining the game's final result. Amusingly, if you visit the websites of the two schools involved, each claims victory. One lists the final score as 80–78, the other as 78–77.

This is one of those rare games people will talk about for a long time.

After the South Lakes High School boys' basketball team won the Virginia state championship in 2024, together with cheering students.

Respect for Rules

November 13, 2020

Last week, I had many sleepless nights. These days, if I do not go to bed at my usual time, it is harder for me to fall asleep—but this time, it was because of the election. Starting Tuesday night, I stayed up every evening watching TV and checking online updates, following the vote count until a winner emerged.

In fact, my sleeplessness began the night before Election Day. On Monday evening, the second game of the Samsung Fire World Baduk (Go) Masters final started at 9 p.m. Eastern Time. It was the second match in a best-of-three final between Korea's top player, 9-dan Shin Jin-Seo, and China's top player, 9-dan Ke Jie. Shin had lost the first game, so he had to win Game 2 to stay in the match.

The game lasted five intense hours. Shin held advantage into the end game but began to lose ground under time pressure and ultimately lost by a mere half-point. I watched the YouTube live stream until the very end, and the defeat left me feeling so frustrated that I could not fall asleep. The loss was especially bitter because Shin had already suffered a questionable defeat in Game 1.

In that first game, Shin Jin-Seo made a "mouse misclick" during the opening moves. Because of COVID-19, the tournament was conducted online, and players had to use a computer mouse to make their moves from their home countries. On his 21st move, Shin accidentally placed a stone on the first line—the edge of the board—an area virtually never played on in the opening. He had intended to play elsewhere, but a mouse malfunction caused the stone to be dropped in the wrong spot.

Everyone watching was shocked. Even Ke Jie, his opponent, froze in disbelief. But Go has a strict rule: once a stone is placed, for any reason, the move cannot be taken back. That is the rule.

Go is a game where even the most absurd mistakes are handled strictly according to the rules. For instance, in modern games, scoring is often done using Chinese rules, where players alternate filling all neutral points (called "dame") after the game ends. In one match, a player accidentally created a "snapback" while filling neutral points, and the opponent captured the stones. Though the mistake was clearly unintentional, the result stood—because the rule is the rule.

In another case, a player placed a stone and then instinctively picked it back up. That is allowed—but the rules require the next move to be placed in the exact same spot. The player forgot and played somewhere else, resulting in a disqualification. In yet another match, a player tried to place a stone, then slid it to another point, violating a newly adopted rule—and again, the result was a loss. No one objected. Everyone agreed: the rules must be strictly upheld.

The recent U.S. presidential election was similarly intense. But now that the vote count has clearly pointed to a winner, I hope all parties will show respect for rules and tradition. Of course, a candidate has the right to file lawsuits. But a lawyer must not bring legal action simply because the client requests it. One of the key ethical responsibilities of a legal professional is to determine whether there is objective evidence to support the client's claims before filing a lawsuit.

That duty falls squarely on the lawyer. Filing suit without sufficient evidence is not part of a legitimate legal process—it is just a tantrum. And the public should never be taken hostage by a tantrum.

Greed and Hatred

January 21, 2022

Not long ago, I felt pleased to hear that two Korean Americans had been appointed as deputy secretaries in Virginia. Although the governor belonged to a different political party than mine, I appreciated that he offered opportunities to members of the Korean American community. I hoped the two appointees would perform well in their new roles.

That news made me reflect on the ambitions I once had for a government post.

My desire first arose eight years ago, just after Governor Terry McAuliffe was elected in Virginia. But calling it a "desire" may be an overstatement, since I did not take any active steps. I suppose I was not that earnest about it in the end.

However, in 2016, my ambition was stronger, and this time I took some concrete steps.

Ahead of that November's presidential election, I thought about my acquaintance with U.S. Senator Tim Kaine, the Democratic vice-presidential candidate, and his wife Anne Holton. Holton had served as Virginia's Secretary of Education and was teaching at George Mason University, located in Fairfax County, Virginia where I was serving as a school board member. She knew me well, too.

Once, while I was chair of the school board, Professor Holton brought her students to observe a meeting. As requested, I met with them during the session to explain the role of the school board and my life stories-how I had immigrated and become an elected member of the school board.

So, before the election, I conveyed to her that I hoped to work in the U.S. Department of Education—specifically as Assistant Secretary for K-12 Education. I also considered the possibility that Holton might be appointed Secretary of Education. She responded positively and suggested we wait until the election was over.

But when the unexpected election results came in, my hopes and efforts vanished in an instant.

My ambition returned in 2017, as the Virginia gubernatorial election approached.

Ralph Northam, then the Lieutenant Governor and expected Democratic nominee, had visited my office in early 2016 while campaigning. I did not want to miss the opportunity. I told him that I was willing to support his campaign and, if he were elected, I hoped to be considered for the position of Secretary of Education.

Because he did not know much about me, I am sure he was taken aback. Of course, I did not expect him to accept my bold proposal on the spot.

The most memorable exchange between us, however, happened two days before the election, in November 2017. That night, Northam was campaigning in Fairfax County, a Democratic stronghold. It was cold, and the rain was pouring. He was giving a speech in a parking lot outside the local Democratic headquarters.

I held my umbrella and did my best to catch his attention. Being short, I pushed through the crowd to move closer. After he finished his speech, I pulled him under my umbrella.

Looking at me, he said,

"Let's talk after the election."

But once elected, he did not keep his word.

I only saw him again in his final year in office—at a Korean American community event I attended only because I wanted to deliver a message on behalf of our community. I had deliberately avoided all other events he was scheduled to attend.

To be fair, I followed the proper process. I applied for the Secretary of Education role immediately after the election and went through the transition team's interview. I was reportedly among the final three or four candidates. So, I cannot say I was given no opportunity at all.

Yet, I could not understand his ultimate choice for the post. He appointed a young Muslim American former middle school teacher and a former noncommissioned officer. But more than anything, what was hardest to forgive was that Governor Northam had gone back on his word to speak with me after the election.

That sense of disappointment and betrayal lingered for a long time.

And I learned that ambition and greed could sometimes give rise to hatred.

Soaked in the rain (November 5, 2017)

Design Defect

September 2, 2022

A few weeks ago, I went on a short vacation to visit my two sons—one living in New York and the other near Boston. I chose to travel by train instead of driving, and thanks to advance booking, the total cost of tickets for the trip—from Washington, D.C., to New York, then to Boston, and back—came to less than $100. As someone who already enjoys train travel, I found this option not only cheaper than gas but also far more pleasant. Watching the scenery roll by, sipping coffee, reading a book, and simply relaxing—this felt like the true way to enjoy a vacation.

To get to the train station in Washington, D.C., I decided to take the Virginia Railway Express (VRE) commuter train for the first time in a while. Though I had installed the ticketing app on my smartphone, I was not familiar enough with it, so I opted to buy my ticket using the vending machine at the station. I arrived ten minutes early to avoid mistakes and carefully followed the on-screen instructions.

First, I touched the screen, selected my destination, entered the number of tickets I wanted, and then inserted my credit card at the final step. It was time for the ticket to be printed. But nothing happened. I waited, puzzled. Something felt off. Then I realized—I had inserted my credit card into the slot where the ticket was supposed to come out.

Now I had to retrieve the card. The problem was that it had gone too far in to grab easily with my fingers. I tried to pinch it out with my thumb and forefinger, but no luck. The fact that I had neatly trimmed my nails for the trip did not help. I looked around for some sort of tool, but of course there was nothing. Making things more awkward was the morning rush—many commuters were around, and I could feel glances thrown my way. I worried about running into someone I knew. Embarrassment washed over me—but I had to get that card out!

Time was running short. The train was arriving soon, and I still had not bought a ticket. Fortunately, another ticket machine stood right next to the first. This time, I made sure to insert the card into the correct slot and successfully purchased a ticket. Now all that remained was to retrieve the card stuck in the first machine. But no matter how hard I tried, I could not grip it. Eventually, the train arrived, and I had to give up.

Left with no other option, I decided that if I could not retrieve the card, I should at least make sure no one else could either. Using my fingertip, I nudged the card further in until it was fully swallowed by the machine. At that point, only a station attendant could have retrieved it.

Even after boarding, I could not stop thinking about that credit card. "I'd better contact the card company and report it lost." Thankfully, I had the credit card app installed on my phone, so canceling the card was not difficult. But when I got to the reason for the report, I hit a snag. None of the options fit this absurd situation. "Of course," I thought, "Who else would make such a ridiculous mistake?" In the end, I chose "Lost" as the reason.

Luckily, a few weeks earlier, my younger son had set up Apple Pay on my phone. Thanks to that, the credit card company quickly issued a new card and linked it to Apple Pay, letting me use it immediately. What a convenient world we live in.

It was only after resolving the card issue that I could breathe easy. Then I reflected on what had happened at the ticket machine. "This was not my fault—it was a design flaw!" Yes, they should have made the ticket output slot and the credit card slot different in shape. The very fact that a card could fit into the ticket slot pointed to a design defect. I remembered the tort law theory from law school: "This is a ground for a class action." A wry smile spread across my face.

But when I later shared the story with my two sons, both gave me a look of disbelief. And then came the punchline:

"Dad, the defective one is not the machine—it is your head. Your head!"

Understanding Differences

November 23, 2011

There was an international student from China with whom I became close when I was in college. At the time, China and the United States had yet to establish formal diplomatic relations, so studying abroad in the U.S. could not have been easy for him. But he was pursuing a Ph.D. on a full scholarship. A graduate of Peking University, he must have been among China's academic elite. He once told me that his childhood dream was to become a world-class table tennis player, and in middle school, he had even been part of China's junior national team. He said he had met Korea's famous player Lee Ailesa as well.

We often talked about a wide range of topics, and one day, we happened to discuss the Korean War. What shocked me was his belief that the war had started with a South Korean invasion of the North. That is what he had learned growing up, and he had never questioned it.

I explained to him that this was not true: "Starting a war requires careful preparation," I said. "If South Korea had attacked first, how could it have lost its capital within just three days? That alone speaks volumes." Even by looking at objective facts, it was clear that the North had initiated the war. He listened and nodded in agreement.

That experience taught me that even someone from China's

most elite circles could view historical facts entirely differently depending on their environment and education. What might be easily refuted by logic alone could still be deeply believed due to differences in information and upbringing. It was a striking realization.

I had a similar experience during recent election season. On the Sunday before Election Day, I received an invitation to speak at two Muslim prayer gatherings. I visited both early that morning.

It turned out these gatherings marked the conclusion of Eid al-Adha, one of Islam's major religious holidays. Not being familiar with Muslim traditions, I had looked up the meaning of the holiday beforehand. I learned it commemorated Ibrahim (Abraham), whom Muslims regard as a patriarch of faith, and his willingness to sacrifice his son out of absolute trust in Allah.

As a Christian, I had grown up hearing the story of Abraham's near sacrifice of his son Isaac to God, so the account was familiar. But what surprised me was what came next.

In Islam, the son Abraham is believed to have offered as a sacrifice was not Isaac, as in Jewish and Christian tradition, but Ishmael, the son of Hagar.

I was taken aback. I had not realized the Islamic tradition could differ so fundamentally from what I had always known. As a school board member in Fairfax County—home to a diverse population in terms of race, culture, and religion—this reminded me of how vital it is to step outside my own small frame of reference to better understand others.

Even within the Korean American community, there are frequent encounters with cultural differences. Consider disputes over labeling the "East Sea" in geography textbooks; the fact that many immigrants from South Vietnam still honor their former national flag despite the fall of Saigon in 1975; controversies over not referring to winter break as "Christmas vacation" in schools; or accommodations for students who miss school to observe religious holidays.

These issues are not simply cultural or religious; they often influence how public policies are developed and implemented. What seems fair from one perspective may not be perceived the same way from another.

We Korean Americans often feel that the mainstream society does not fully understand us—and to some extent, that is true. But this also means we must strive to understand those who come from backgrounds different from our own.

I believe that when we take the first step in understanding others, we earn the right to ask for that same effort in return. And the more we expand our understanding of each other's differences, the stronger and healthier our community will become.

Comedy Club

September 30, 2022

A month or two ago, I visited my younger son who lives in New York. Since he was in his thirties now, I thought about what we could do together and decided on an outdoor performance in Central Park and a visit to a comedy club. The outdoor show was my idea, but the comedy club was his suggestion. It was my first time watching a performance in Central Park, and the comedy club visit was only my second ever—the first being many years ago when my older son was in college. I booked the tickets for the performance, and my younger son handled the comedy club reservation.

When we arrived at the comedy club, a long line of people waiting to enter made me a little anxious. But thankfully, those with reservations had a separate line, and only a few people had arrived before us. Once the doors opened, the reserved guests were admitted first. The usher asked if we had a seat preference: "Do you want to sit in the front row?" I hesitated briefly, but my son quickly said, "Yes." The front row—was that really a good idea? The last time I came with my older son, we sat in the back and enjoyed the show at ease. But it was too late. The decision was made.

Our seats were front and center—just a few feet from the stage and directly in front of the comedians. A wave of worry came over me. Comics often interact with the audience, and we were prime targets for their jokes. Oh well. I opened the menu and ordered something. I was hungry, and each person could order two items with the admission ticket—one food and one drink. When the food came, I started eating.

The show began. The first comedian took the stage and asked where the audience members were from. People responded with various places. Eventually, he got to me. I think he expected me to say "Korea," but I answered, "Virginia, Fairfax." The comedian shot back, "Is that not a super racist place?" and laughter erupted all around.

As I kept eating during the show, I noticed we might have been the only ones doing so in the front row—others just sipped drinks. Then one comedian looked at me and asked, "Is the food good?" Oops. I had probably been too focused on eating and not making eye contact. From a comedian's perspective, the audience's visual engagement is key. Still, I replied, "Yes, it is good. I was hungry," which drew a big laugh. But after that, I found it hard to keep eating. Darn, I still had more to go. I decided to stop.

A few more comedians came up. Then one of them asked about the man sitting next to me—my younger son. "Is he your son? Or... someone you are in a relationship with?" I froze. What kind of question was that? He was implying we might be a gay couple. I paused, then responded, "Second boy." The comedian quipped, "That's not a real answer," and turned to my son. But he just smiled. "He won't answer either?" More laughter. Sitting in the front row was clearly a mistake.

The show went on, but then yet another comedian came up and asked the same question again. What is this? Why are they that curious? I had to answer once more. Everyone seemed to be holding their breath, waiting for my response. "My... second... son." The room erupted in applause. The comedian looked confused, but the clapping continued for a while. I stood, waved my right hand, and gave small bows to the front, sides, and back.

As we exited after the show, a woman and her daughter approached and said, "Thanks to you, we had an even better time tonight." What do you say to that? I just mumbled, "Well, that is how comedy clubs are, I guess."

Later, I heard from my son that he had wanted to bury his head in the ground that night. Our visit to the comedy club was a comedy of its own.

ChatGPT said: It is a club located at 117 MacDougal Street in Manhattan, New York.

Sitting in the front row.

Reflecting on Thanksgiving

November 29, 2013

Every Thanksgiving, one particular memory always comes to mind.

When I first immigrated to the U.S. and started high school, I remember how, after Thanksgiving break, classmates and teachers would greet me with the same question:

"Did you have turkey?"

During the three years I attended high school in the U.S., I do not recall ever eating turkey at home. When our family first arrived some 40 years ago, we did not find turkey to be all that tasty. The only time I tried it was in the school cafeteria, where it was served before Thanksgiving. At home, our holiday meals usually featured chicken or ham instead. So, whenever I was asked "Did you have turkey?" after the holiday, I struggled to answer.

Even now, I do not think turkey is particularly delicious. But I have become used to such questions and, more broadly, to American life and the culture surrounding Thanksgiving. And when I think about the meaning of this holiday, it feels like more than just a day for food. It is a day to be thankful—or at least, to reflect on what we can be thankful for.

Looking back, I realize I have much to be grateful for this past year.

Not everything went the way I hoped, and I could not do everything I wanted. But despite that, I am thankful to God, in whom I believe, for having watched over me and carried me this far. If I had to pick one thing I am most thankful for, it would be simply that I have been given the gift of life to this day.

Twelve years ago, I underwent surgery for colon cancer.

At the time, I had been experiencing persistent stomach pain, but I brushed it off as indigestion. I delayed getting a proper checkup and ended up allowing the illness to progress. I was in my mid-forties then, still considered young, and had unfounded confidence in my health. But by the time I was diagnosed, the tumor had grown to the size of a golf ball. My colon was at risk of rupturing, and I needed immediate surgery.

It was my first major surgery. I could not help but think about the possibility of death. Before entering the operating room, I prayed with a desperate heart. My children were still young, and my youngest had just finished fourth grade. I prayed to God: "Please let me live at least until he enters college." I felt I needed to be there as a father at least until then.

Thankfully, the surgery was a success. About a foot length of my colon was removed, but the cancer had not spread. The doctor still recommended six months of chemotherapy, just to be on the side of caution. Since then, every follow-up exam has shown no signs of recurrence, and I have been able to stay healthy. I became a cancer survivor.

Now, twelve years later, my youngest has not only entered college but has graduated and gone on to graduate school. The eight years I prayed for have long passed, and I have been granted four more years beyond that. In some ways, these past four years feel like bonus time. That is why I try to live each day with gratitude. Because these are extra days, I cherish them all the more and try to live each one to the fullest.

Another thing I am thankful for is my optimistic nature.

I tend to face challenges with a positive outlook rather than a negative one. When hard times come, I try to think, "It could have been worse—let's be grateful that it was not." I do not know if I was born this way or if I learned it through experience, but being able to hold onto gratitude is one of my greatest blessings.

Someone once said, "Hope is even more frightening than fear."

That might sound strange at first, but I interpret it differently. To me, it means, "Hope is the strength that allows us to overcome all difficulties." When hardship strikes, I am thankful that it did not lead to something worse. And above all, I am thankful that I can still have hope.

So, this Thanksgiving, I would like to say to you:

"Did you have turkey?"

And one more thing—I hope that you have had even more reasons to be thankful than I have. And may those blessings continue until next Thanksgiving. Even if tough times come your way, I hope you hold on to a positive spirit and never let go of hope.

A photo taken with my sons the day before surgery, capturing the last image of my healthy abdomen.

Chapter 2
Immigration Life

Introduction

It has now been over 50 years since I began living as an immigrant in the United States. My entire family immigrated together when I was in high school, and the time I have spent living here is more than three times longer than the time I lived in my homeland. When we arrived at Dulles Airport near Washington, D.C., at the end of August 1974, the old white used car[5] that my father—who had come to the U.S. a year earlier as an employment-based immigrant—brought to pick us up looked incredibly impressive to me. That car needed two cans of engine oil every week just to keep running, and I thought all cars required that much oil.

Sometimes, when I tell other Korean immigrants how long I have lived in the U.S., they look surprised. I am not sure whether it is because the number of years is so long, or because they expect that someone who has lived here that long would be indistinguishable from an American—yet I am not. And when I tell Americans I have lived here for over 50 years, they may also be surprised, though perhaps for a different reason: despite all those years, I still speak English with a strong accent.

For thirty of those 50 years, I devoted much of my time to public service and community work. To other immigrants, I may seem like someone who has achieved the American Dream

---

5) The car was a Plymouth from around 1967, and he said he had bought it for just a few hundred dollars.

and blended well into mainstream society. Perhaps I have even tried to appear that way in my own way. But I still find myself introducing myself as an immigrant, which likely reflects the fact that there are still aspects of life in America that feel unfamiliar or uncomfortable. Perhaps this is the life I have chosen. Thinking of it that way brings me some comfort.

At the same time, as Dr. Sang Hyun Lee[6] once argued, perhaps I should be grateful for the special role given to immigrants—who often find themselves living on the margins—in contributing creatively to the development of the community. Still, I have a hope that my two American-born sons, my only granddaughter, and any future descendants will not have to live lives as people on the margins. Perhaps hope is a form of self-denial, but I cannot help but have it.

---

[6] Dr. Sang Hyun Lee (1938-2023) was a world-renowned scholar who taught systematic theology for 31 years at Princeton Theological Seminary in the United States, where he was the first Asian professor in the school's history. Born in Sangju, North Gyeongsang Province, he graduated from Daegu's Keisung High School and left for the United States in 1955 at the age of 17 to study abroad in New Jersey. He earned his undergraduate degree from Worcester College and received his doctorate from Harvard University with a dissertation on the theology of Jonathan Edwards. He was named Professor Emeritus upon his retirement in 2011.

The Reverend Jae Hoon Park

August 6, 2021

"Jesus, my true desire, my dearest friend is He,
How beautiful is the Lord, my Savior dear to me.
Like a lily of the valley, like the morning star so bright,
No words can fully tell of His glorious light.

When my heart is troubled, He is my greatest peace,
When my soul is lonely, His friendship does not cease.
He is the lily of the valley, the bright and morning star—
There is nothing on this earth that compares to who You are."

These are some of the lyrics from the hymn "He is the Lily of the Valley," arranged by The Reverend Jae. I always loved this hymn. Back in high school in Korea, whenever two younger girls at church youth group sang a duet of this piece, I found myself completely drawn in. The beauty of the music, the depth of the lyrics, and even the girls' appearance and voices—all of it captivated me. I felt the same years later during my college days when I attended a Korean church near Boston. Two female students from a prestigious nearby women's college would occasionally sing the same hymn as a duet, and it brought back the same feelings I had as a high schooler.

Then I heard the news that The Reverend Jae had passed away.

He founded the Light Presbyterian Church, one of the largest Korean churches in Toronto, and served as its founding senior pastor. Until his passing, he held the title of pastor emeritus. Living to the age of ninety-nine, his life was surely a blessed one. His music and life profoundly influenced many, so one could say he lived a life that lacked nothing. And yet, the fact that another great elder has left us fills me with an inescapable sense of emptiness.

Though I never had a personal conversation with Reverend Park, I did see him up close once—probably in the spring of 1979 as I recall. However, since he reportedly moved to Toronto in 1979, it might have been in 1980 or 1981.

At that time, Reverend Park brought the Toronto Korean Choir to perform in the Boston area. Most of the choir members appeared to be middle-aged or older. I do not remember the full program, but it included not only sacred music but also Korean folk songs and lyric songs. For one or two pieces, the Boston Korean Choir joined in. That group was made up of members from various Korean church choirs in the area, and since I was active in my church choir, I was invited to participate. The Boston choir was conducted by Professor Ingul Ivan Oak,[7] who

---

7) Professor Ingul Ivan Oak (Professor Emeritus at the University of Massachusetts Lowell) earned both his diploma and master's degree from the New England Conservatory of Music and has won multiple awards and performed in collaboration with world-renowned competitions. He served as a vocal coach for the Harvard University Glee Club and worked for 32 years at the University of Massachusetts Lowell as Chair of the Voice Department and Opera Director.

was then on the voice faculty at Lowell University. He must be over ninety by now.

During the joint rehearsal with the visiting Toronto choir, I heard something I will never forget. Several choir members, I was told, worked as worm catchers. They said worms had to be caught at night. I had never even heard of such a job, and it came as a shock. Learning that many Koreans in Toronto did this kind of work showed me just how difficult immigrant life in Canada was at the time.

Of course, life for Korean immigrants in the U.S. was not easy either. Many, like my own mother, worked as cleaners. Jobs at convenience stores like 7-Eleven or High's were considered relatively stable. Women with good hand skills worked all day doing keypunch data entry.

For Korean immigrants in Toronto who lived such difficult lives, Reverend Park offered comfort and encouragement through choral music. Simply being able to gather and sing must have been a great joy. After the Boston concert, the Toronto group boarded a bus back on Sunday evening, without much sightseeing. They had to catch worms again the next day. Watching them leave, I felt an ache in my heart.

To Reverend Park, who served as a social, musical, and spiritual leader for over forty years to those very people—I want to finally say thank you. Thanks to your music and your dedication, many found comfort and hope. Though this comes late, I offer my deepest gratitude once again.

A Seat at the Table

November 8, 2019

There is an English expression, "a seat at the table." Literally, it means "a place to sit at the table," but its real meaning is "a chance to participate in the decision-making process." Public officials elected in this Tuesday's election ultimately gained such seats. To occupy a seat at the table—especially when representing a specific group—also signifies that the group is being recognized as having a voice in shaping decisions.

After attending a recent meeting about how Fairfax County allocates public funds, I was once again reminded that our Korean American community must continue to advocate for such seats.

Of Fairfax County's annual budget, about $900 million is dedicated to health and human services. Roughly $13 million of that is distributed through a fund known as the Consolidated Community Funding Pool (CCFP). This fund supports projects planned by nonprofit and community organizations to benefit Fairfax County residents.

The CCFP is allocated every two years, and funded projects must include plans covering two years of activity. In the 2019–2020 fiscal cycle, projects ranged from receiving as little as $20,000 (for emergency food assistance) to as much as $670,000 (for a program helping ex-offenders and their families reintegrate into society). The Korean Community Service Center of Greater Washington has also received CCFP support for key initiatives.

What brought the issue of representation into sharp focus for me was the absence of any Korean American representatives on the policy advisory body that helps guide how these funds are used. Among nearly twenty advisory members, not a single one represented the Korean American community.

Of course, members of such advisory committees must consider the needs of the entire county. However, in order to reflect the unique concerns of various minority communities within the county, it is essential to have a representative who can articulate the perspectives and needs of Korean Americans. If we want our voices included and our community's needs reflected in funding decisions, we must be present at those tables.

In particular, we need more active Korean American participation in bodies like the Selection Advisory Committee, which has significant influence in deciding who receives funding. Some may wonder whether a single voice could make a difference. But based on my past experience reviewing funding applications for United Way, I can say that even one dissenting voice is not easily dismissed. Every committee member's opinion is respected during deliberations, and efforts are made to incorporate differing perspectives.

Unfortunately, applications for the 2021–2022 Selection Advisory Committee closed at the end of August. However, since the committee is reconstituted every two years, I hope many from our community will consider applying next time.

There are many areas in our local community where we

can participate and contribute. Sometimes we miss out simply because we are unaware of the opportunities. In such cases, we can ask our district supervisors or city council members, or community organizations such as Korean associations to take the lead in identifying these openings.

Local government policies and actions directly affect our daily lives. If we want the Korean American community to be recognized and influential, we must actively engage. Let us not miss our rightful "seat at the table."

Meeting My 40-Year Juniors

July 14, 2017

A few weeks ago, I met two students who are forty years my junior at the university I attended. Strictly speaking, it has not been 40 years since I graduated—only 36—so they are not exactly my juniors by four decades just yet. But the students entering college this year will be graduating in four years, and only then will they officially become my 40-year juniors.

The meeting came about through a fellow school board member. She contacted me and said that two students from a high school in her district had been accepted to my alma mater and suggested that it might be nice for me to meet them over breakfast and share some words of experience as an alum. She thought it would be meaningful since both students were from minority backgrounds and might be encouraged by meeting someone like me. I was not sure how useful my distant memories would be to them, but I made time on a Saturday morning, hoping I could at least be of some support.

One of the students came from a middle-class family. The other was the youngest of six siblings. His parents were still living in the country where he was born, while he had been living in the U.S. with his brothers and sisters. He had come to the U.S. at around age six, so he spoke English fluently, but it was easy to sense that he had grown up in a modest, financially constrained household without his parents.

This student, who came from a difficult background, showed up dressed in what seemed to be a brand-new outfit—perhaps feeling nervous about having breakfast at a country club with two school board members and the school principal. But his lack of adult guidance was visible even in his appearance. Though he wore new clothes, the fabric still bore fold marks from being just out of the package, not yet ironed. It looked as if he had hastily prepared the night before. That moment brought back vivid memories of my own immigration experience when we came to the U.S. after struggling to get by in Korea.

Back in high school in Korea, I barely had any proper casual clothes. I wore my school uniforms to both school and church, and at home I wore gym clothes or military-style training clothes. Just before immigrating to the U.S., I was finally able to get one or two sets of casual clothes. But even after arriving in the U.S., things were not much better. We could not afford new clothes, so I wore items bought at cheap stores or secondhand shops.

I remember once, a classmate asked me, "Do you only have one outfit?"

He liked the light green top I had brought from Korea and thought I kept wearing it on purpose. But in reality, it was the only decent piece of clothing I had. So, when it got dirty, I would wash it and wear it again the next day. Even after I gained weight in the U.S. and the shirt became tight, I had no choice but to keep wearing it.

Another time, a group of school friends unexpectedly came to visit my apartment. They were white classmates I was close to, and since I had never invited them over before, they must have been curious. I was completely caught off guard. I did not want to show them the modest conditions we lived in. In the end, we just stood outside the door and chatted briefly before I sent them off.

But I imagine they must have caught a glimpse over my shoulder when I opened the door—a worn-out sofa set; a bed placed in the living room due to a lack of bedrooms. I am sure it looked unfamiliar to them. At the time, immigrants were not as common, and white students likely had no idea how different an immigrant family's living conditions could be from theirs.

To these two students, especially the one growing up in hardship, I wanted to say: do not let yourself feel small or intimidated in college. Stand tall and pursue your studies with pride. I shared some of my own past experiences—how I once lost confidence, and how that prevented me from having a more active and fulfilling college life. Sometimes I spoke with humor, sometimes with seriousness. The students listened intently.

Watching them, I suddenly realized: I had officially become one of those long-winded senior alumni.

Teaching Our Roots

March 23, 2018

Last Saturday, I attended a spring festival held by a Vietnamese language school in Falls Church, Virginia. The school operates much like our Korean language schools, teaching Vietnamese language and culture to students of Vietnamese heritage. It appeared to be running out of a borrowed church space. Though I could not stay long, the visit left a lasting impression.

Thanks to the organizers, I was seated next to the president of the local Vietnamese community association. Throughout the event, he offered helpful explanations. Most of the program was conducted in Vietnamese, so without his commentary, I would have had trouble understanding much of it.

The president appeared to be in his late seventies. He shared that he came to the U.S. as a refugee after the fall of Saigon in 1975. He recalled how, during his early years in America, he learned how to build a new life from Korean immigrants. One Korean man he knew worked in siding and was, in his words, incredibly hardworking—able to finish an entire house in just two days with the help of one other worker. They would start before dawn and continue working until after dark. He was deeply impressed by their dedication. The Korean man's wife had trained as a beautician and worked in a salon. That couple, he said, became his role models. Inspired by them, he pursued painting as his trade, while his own wife also learned cosmetology and found work, helping them establish their new life.

One thing that caught my eye at the festival was a flag flying beside the American flag. But it was not the flag of unified Vietnam—it was the flag of former South Vietnam. After the U.S. national anthem was played, the attendees, led by students, sang the national anthem of the defunct South Vietnam. These Vietnamese American children, born in the U.S., were not being taught the flag and anthem of unified Vietnam, but rather those of South Vietnam—symbols of their cultural roots. The community association president spoke firmly, saying he could never accept the current communist regime.

One segment of the event featured a lengthy explanation for students about the Tet Offensive of 1968. "Tet" is the Vietnamese term for Lunar New Year. The Vietnam War had dragged on since 1955, but the Tet Offensive marked a turning point. During a supposed two-day ceasefire for the New Year, the North Vietnamese army and Viet Cong launched a surprise attack across South Vietnam. The ensuing battles lasted for months, with both sides suffering heavy casualties. For the American public, it shattered the illusion that the war was nearing a successful conclusion. Until then, many believed the U.S. was gaining the upper hand, but the offensive made it clear that peace was far from reach. This event fueled a dramatic surge in antiwar sentiment across the U.S.

Eventually, the United States decided to withdraw from the war, and South Vietnam fell in 1975. The festival placed particular emphasis on the Battle of Huế. Located about fifty kilometers south of the dividing line between North and South Vietnam, Huế saw a month-long battle during which the North Vietnamese and Viet Cong reportedly massacred thousands of South Vietnamese civilians. The community president recounted that the attackers were so ruthless that, to save bullets, they used spears to kill people. The horror of this reminded me of the atrocities I had learned about as a child in Korea during the Korean War. I found it striking how these Vietnamese American children were being taught such painful history as a way of remembering their ancestral homeland.

As I left the event, I could not help but reflect on the state of Korean "roots education" in our own community. What, and how, should we be teaching our future generations? Alongside Korean language instruction, how can we pass down Korean history and identity? If we were to create a standardized curriculum that our diaspora could embrace, what should it include?

And if Korea is someday reunified, how should future generations of Korean Americans learn and interpret post-1945 Korean history? Will we, like the Vietnamese community, emphasize one side's narrative? Or will we strive to offer a more balanced view that helps our youth understand history with perspective?

These questions lingered in my mind as I left, turning the day into one of reflection—and reminding me of the deep responsibility we bear in shaping identity and history education for the generations to come.

Korean Language School Washington Area (Virginia and Maryland) Council's Vocabulary Contest and Academic Presentation (May 3, 2025)

Giving a lecture to parents

Senior Citizen Student

June 25, 1999
Washington Media

As in previous years, I attended several high school graduation ceremonies this year. Last Saturday evening, I was at the Thomas Jefferson High School for Science and Technology graduation held at the Patriot Center at George Mason University, where Vice President Al Gore gave the commencement address. Although the tight security presence was somewhat distracting, it was still worth it for the rare opportunity to see the Vice President in person.

On Monday afternoon, Annandale High School held its ceremony at Constitution Hall in D.C., while Robinson High School used its own gymnasium for the event. The keynote speaker at Robinson was Janet Hill, wife of famous professional football player Calvin Hill and mother of NBA star Grant Hill. Among the ten pieces of advice she offered graduates, what stood out most was her emphasis that "listening to your mother" was the most important.

That same evening, I also attended Fairfax High School's graduation, followed by Lake Braddock Secondary School and Pimmit Hills Alternative High School the next day. On Thursday, I joined the Adult High School graduation held at Woodson High School. I offer heartfelt congratulations to all the graduates and their families who supported them.

But of all the ceremonies I attended, the one that left the deepest impression on me was the graduation for the External Diploma Program (EDP) held last Tuesday evening at Falls Church High School.

The External Diploma Program is one of three programs offered by Fairfax County Public Schools to help adults over the age of twenty-one earn a high school diploma. Though it requires modest tuition, the program allows adult learners who did not finish high school to complete their studies at their own pace. Most learning is done at home, and enrollment is open year-round. Interestingly, participants in the program are referred to as "clients" rather than students. Many are married and have children, and some even keep their enrollment secret from their employers, children, or neighbors due to the stigma they feel about not having graduated high school. As a result, some chose not to attend the ceremony, and their names were omitted from the program.

The ages of the graduates ranged from 19 to 66. One graduate, a 66-year-old African American woman with thirteen grandchildren and five great-grandchildren, had retired in 1991 and enrolled in the program at age 65 to pursue an unfulfilled dream. She shared her plans to continue her education that fall at Northern Virginia Community College (NOVA),[8] where she intended to study religious studies and communications. Surrounded by her family,

---

8) Northern Virginia Community College, also known as NOVA, is a two-year college with campuses located in six different areas throughout Northern Virginia.

she celebrated her graduation in what could only be described as a beautiful and moving moment.

Among the graduates was one Korean student, 51 years old. After arriving in the U.S. in 1989, he worked weekdays as a custodian in Fairfax County Public Schools and spent weekends and holidays at Fairfax Hospital, delivering bed linens. He had worked every single day of the year without a break. Hoping for the day he could work a full-time job with regular hours at a single location, he began with adult ESL classes four years ago, and now, finally, he earned his high school diploma. He credited the constant support and encouragement from his wife and college-aged daughter.

This student explained that his goal was not only to get a better job or further his education, but also to serve as an example for his daughter—demonstrating the importance of perseverance and valuing education. Despite physical fatigue, he remained dedicated to his studies and consistently served as a model of diligence to his fellow students. Hearing teachers express sincere praise for this older Korean student, I could not help but offer a deep and respectful round of applause from the bottom of my heart.

To anyone who has not yet earned a high school diploma but wishes to challenge themselves, I strongly recommend considering this program. It came as no surprise that this late-blooming student received a special award at the ceremony.

Congratulations, Mr. Lee!

Adult high school graduation ceremony (photo provided by Fairfax County Public Schools)

Ramadan Dinner

July 25, 2014

Last Friday, I had the opportunity to attend an iftar dinner hosted by the Turkish American Friendship Association. Iftar refers to the evening meal during the Islamic holy month of Ramadan, when Muslims break their daily fast. Though I had previously attended a few iftar gatherings at mosques, this was my first time being invited by this particular organization.

I am a Christian. However, in my role as a school board member, I believe that understanding the diverse communities in our area requires going beyond my own religious background. Engaging with people whose religion, philosophy, or political views differ from mine is unavoidable—and sometimes, persuasion is necessary. But understanding must come first. That is why I welcome such opportunities and gladly accept invitations like this. Just as I value my freedom of religion and belief, others deserve the same freedom.

I learned a lot from this dinner. For Muslims, Ramadan is the holiest month. It is the ninth month of the Islamic calendar, which, like the traditional Korean lunar calendar, is based on the moon. However, unlike in Korea, where leap months are used to align the calendar with the solar year, Muslims make no such adjustment. As a result, Ramadan shifts about 10 to 11 days earlier each year in the Gregorian calendar, cycling through all seasons over time.

This year, Ramadan lasted from June 28 to July 27 and ended this past Sunday. During Ramadan, Muslims fast from before sunrise until sunset each day. Not even a sip of water is allowed. So, when Ramadan falls in the summer, the long daylight hours make fasting even more difficult. That Friday evening, the meal did not begin until after 8:40 p.m. Since sunrise was before 6:00 a.m., that meant nearly 15 hours without food or drink.

Before dinner, an Islamic cleric led a prayer. It was a traditional Islamic prayer, and for the guests, a translated version was provided on screen. The prayer included references to Muhammad and his relationship with God (Allah). After the prayer, I offered my own prayer in my own way. But I could not help wondering: how do non-Christians feel when they encounter Christian prayers at Korean community events? Perhaps they feel the same way I did when hearing the Islamic prayer that evening.

Listening to the cleric's explanation, I found that the meaning of fasting during Ramadan had elements I could fully relate to as a Christian. He explained that fasting was not just physical practice but also a spiritual one.

Physically, it involves abstaining from food and drink, which encourages empathy for the poor and hungry. That is why charitable giving is especially emphasized during Ramadan. In fact, charity is one of the five core pillars of Islam, along with fasting.

The spiritual discipline was also moving. The cleric said that everything we ate and drank was not our possession but a gift from God (Allah), and the act of refraining from consuming it before the appointed time was a form of reverence. Although all the food was already served on the table by 8:00 p.m., no one touched it until the designated sunset time. The message was clear: food may be within reach, but it is not to be eaten until God permits it.

This teaching resonated deeply with me as a Christian as well. It reminded me that food is not just a means of survival, but a symbol of divine grace.

Through that evening meal and my interactions with Muslims, I was once again reminded how much we could learn from people of different faiths. Even between religions that sometimes view each other with hostility, there are shared values and points of empathy. Recognizing our differences and approaching one another with an open heart is essential. And yes—the food that night was also excellent.

Chapter 3
Education Stories

Introduction

If there is any field to which I have devoted more time and passion than my 30-year legal career, it would undoubtedly be education. I began serving as an appointed school board member in 1995, just six months before the position became elected. Since then, I have run for office eight times—losing twice and winning six elections—and I currently serve as a six-term member on the school board.

Though the role is not considered a full-time job, the workload often exceeds that of one. The compensation is modest—more an allowance than a salary—but the responsibilities are substantial. In Fairfax County, where I reside, the school board has final authority over all matters concerning the county's public schools. It hires and, when necessary, dismisses the superintendent. It also provides direction to and oversight of superintendent, in addition to setting policies and budgets. It operates as a collective leadership body of twelve members, with the superintendent functioning as a contracted professional executive.

It is rare to find a Korean American who does not have strong opinions about education. The emphasis placed on gaining admission to a prestigious university is strikingly similar to what we see in Korea, though perhaps differing in intensity. I, too, have developed my own views and convictions on education and college admissions. Having completed high school, college, and law school in the U.S.—and having raised two children who also went through the American school system—I have gained a perspective shaped by direct experience. Yet, I make no claim to have all the answers. I can only speak to what I have personally seen and lived.

Even so, I write columns for newspapers and broadcast outlets, give lectures, and now publish this book because I possess a unique blend of firsthand experience, knowledge, and insight. If the educational stories and reflections I share here prompt readers—even those who may not fully agree—to pause and reflect, then I will consider this work to have fulfilled its purpose.

Ladder of Social Mobility

September 27, 2019

Former Supreme Court Justice Kim Young-Ran, Korea's first female justice, recently remarked in a press conference that "a society where dragons no longer rise from humble creeks cannot prosper," and that "the ladder of social mobility seems to be narrowing." She warned that "this ladder must not be kicked away, blocked, or made narrower." She also noted, "Ours has been a highly educated society compared to others, with relatively easier mobility and a strong desire for advancement—but with that, also a deep sense of frustration."

These remarks have resonated more strongly in light of the controversy surrounding the alleged preferential treatment given to the children of Minister of Justice Cho Kuk surfaced during his confirmation hearings. Whether the allegations are true or constitute legal violations will be determined through criminal proceedings. Even if these issues are not directly tied to his official duties, they have become matters of public concern—and the truth must be fully revealed.

Yet, I view the concept of a "ladder of upward mobility" with some reservation. The phrase assumes that social classes exist in the first place. Without classes, there would be no need to speak of "moving up." The very notion of "upward" carries an implicit value judgment—suggesting that moving up is desirable, while moving down is not. But what exactly do we mean by "social class"?

In the Joseon Dynasty, society was rigidly divided into official status groups—scholars, farmers, artisans, and merchants. But in modern Korea, there is no such legally defined class system. So, what then determines class today? Is it one's occupation, wealth, public respect, or admiration? Or is it a combination of these factors?

For instance, if a primary or secondary school teacher becomes a university professor, is that considered upward mobility? If a professor becomes a legislator or a cabinet minister, is that another step up? Conversely, if someone's business fails, is that a fall down off the ladder? How many rungs did they lose? People will have different answers. And even if we could agree on what constitutes a class, how should we value movement between classes? More importantly, should a child's education focus on climbing upward at all?

As a school board member for the past 20 years, I have always encouraged students to do their best. I have advised them to attend college if they have the opportunity. But not as a means to elevate their social class. Rather, I believe in developing one's abilities and using them meaningfully and responsibly.

There is no hierarchy among occupations. As members of society, we simply play different roles. If everyone became a doctor or lawyer, who would cook our meals or repair our roofs? We need bus drivers, police officers, bank tellers, and grocery store cashiers. A person's worth should be measured not by their title or income, but by how faithfully they carry out their role with the talents and circumstances they are given. No job is inherently superior to another. I hope parents and educators alike will keep this in mind when guiding the next generation.

The same goes for wealth. Earning money is not wrong, nor must one seek poverty for its own sake. But when wealth becomes the measuring stick for status or class, the moral foundation of society begins to erode. Of course, a basic standard of living is essential. But a lack of economic abundance should not be equated with being "lower" on the social ladder.

Personally, I have never liked the phrase, "a dragon rising from a creek," which is commonly used to describe someone from a humble background achieving great success. If "creek" implies something lowly or shameful, then the phrase is an insult to the person's family.

College Acceptance Notifications

April 5, 2024

Thursday, March 28 was a highly significant day for students planning to begin college this fall. That evening, several of the most selective universities—including members of the Ivy League—released their regular decision results. Among them were Harvard, Yale, and Princeton, as well as Stanford, the University of Chicago, Northwestern, and Duke.

Some students had already secured college admissions through early decision or early action, but they were a minority. Many others, despite having received offers from excellent institutions, anxiously checked their emails that evening, hoping for good news from slightly more prestigious schools. It was a moment of heightened tension not only for students but for their parents and families as well. Given the extremely low acceptance rates, disappointment was common—but the hope of hearing even one "yes" felt akin to awaiting a lottery win.

I, too, had been anticipating the day. My own children finished school long ago, but I was eager to learn the outcomes for students I had interviewed as an alumni interviewer for my alma mater. Each year, I interview only a few applicants, and as I did last year, I submitted a strong recommendation for one of them. While all the students I interviewed were exceptional and deserving, I carefully selected one candidate for recommendation, knowing that the acceptance rate was under 4%.

I even rearranged my schedule to attend the regional alumni interviewer meeting where we discuss standout applicants, despite it overlapping with a school board session. At the meeting, I emphasized how I had come straight from another commitment to express my support for this student. And yet, for the second year in a row, the student I recommended was not admitted. I am sure the student was disappointed—and I was, too.

At my alma mater, alumni interviewers do not have access to applicants' transcripts or recommendation letters. We also may not ask directly about academic performance. Thus, our assessments must be based solely on a brief conversation—typically about an hour long—and the impressions formed from it. Naturally, this limits the depth of evaluation we can offer.

Still, when I recall the earnest hopes of these students during our interviews, it is hard not to feel heartbroken. What is more, the admissions office prohibits interviewers from contacting students who were not admitted. This is likely a precaution to avoid any potential legal issues stemming from follow-up communication—even if it is simply meant to encourage or console.

Every year around this time, I find myself wanting to share a message with the parents of college applicants. When a student does not receive the acceptance he hoped for, the person most affected is often the student himself. And in many cases, students already have a clear sense of why things did not work out. This is not the time for parents or others to make things harder.

In particular, remarks like "If only you had studied harder" or "If only that one test score had been better" are not helpful. Students are already aware of where they may have fallen short, and no amount of hindsight commentary will change the outcome. What they need now is affirmation of their efforts and reassurance that even if the result was not ideal, there are still many opportunities ahead—and that they can thrive wherever they go.

College admissions season is inevitably a stressful time for students and families alike. But rather than letting disappointment and regret cast a longer shadow than necessary, I hope everyone can get through this period with grace, mutual support, and encouragement.

To all the students and families who navigated this year's admissions journey—and to all those who stood quietly by them in support—I offer my heartfelt congratulations and encouragement.

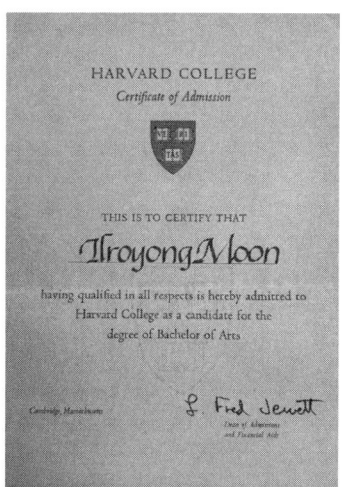

I no longer have the actual acceptance letter, only this certificate. However, the spelling of my name—written carefully by hand—was incorrect. It should have been spelled "Ilryong."

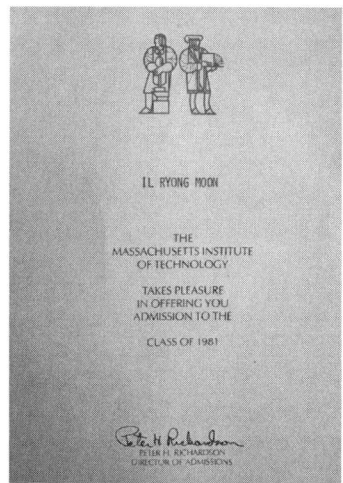

Here too, the "IL" and "RYONG" in my name were separated. Because of its difficult spelling, it often causes confusion.

Hail Mary

November 1, 2024

I often hear the expression "Hail Mary." Originally from a Catholic prayer asking the Virgin Mary for help, the phrase has come to refer to last-ditch efforts—most commonly in sports, but also in business, politics, and personal life—where one makes a bold, often desperate move in hopes of a dramatic success.

Two recent sports events brought this expression vividly to mind. The first was at last week's renaming ceremony for Woodson High School in Fairfax County. The school, formerly named after W.T. Woodson, is now known as Carter G. Woodson High School. Though it is still called "Woodson," the name now honors a quite different figure. W.T. Woodson was Fairfax County's superintendent from 1929 to 1961 and a staunch opponent of school desegregation. Carter G. Woodson, by contrast, was the son of formerly enslaved parents, entered high school at age 20, graduated in just two years, and went on to earn a Ph.D. from Harvard. He later became the dean of the College of Arts and Sciences at Howard University and a pioneer in the field of African American history.

Among the speakers at the renaming ceremony was a former coach who led the Woodson boys' basketball team for 35 years, beginning in 1962. During his remarks, he mentioned Tommy Amaker, a Woodson graduate who played for Duke University, later served as an assistant coach there, and went on to head coaching roles at Seton Hall and the University of Michigan. He now coaches the men's basketball team at Harvard.

I personally witnessed Amaker's final high school game in 1983, when Woodson faced off against my alma mater, T.C. Williams High School,[9] in the Northern Virginia regional championship. With just four seconds left on the clock, T.C. scored to take a two-point lead. Amaker got the ball, sped down the court, and launched a shot from midcourt—a true Hail Mary. The ball went in, but the referee ruled that the shot had left his hand just after the buzzer. The shot was disallowed, and the T.C. crowd, me included, let out a huge sigh of relief.

The second "Hail Mary" moment came during last Sunday's professional football game between the Washington and Chicago teams. As a Washington fan, I watched anxiously. Up through the third quarter, Washington had controlled the game but had only scored through four field goals—no touchdowns. Despite several drives deep into Chicago territory, they failed to finish.

Then, just as I feared, Chicago struck. With 43 seconds remaining, they scored a touchdown to close the gap to 12–7. Just 18 seconds later, they scored again—another touchdown and a two-point conversion—bringing the score to 15–12 in their favor. Washington had one last chance. To tie the game, they needed at least a field goal—but with only 2 seconds left and the ball at

---

9) The name of T.C. Williams High School was also changed in 2021 to Alexandria City High School. T.C. Williams had served for many years as superintendent in the city of Alexandria, where the school is located, but he had opposed racial integration.

their own 48-yard line, they were far out of range.

There was only one option: a long pass. As the quarterback dodged defenders to buy time, receivers ran toward the end zone. From about thirty-five yards out, he launched the ball. It grazed the fingertips of several players in front of the end zone before a Washington receiver caught it in the end zone. Touchdown! In the final second, Washington pulled off an 18–15 comeback victory.

What mattered most in that moment was that this Hail Mary pass was not a wild gamble based purely on luck. The team had practiced this scenario over and over. The odds were low—but it was no blind hope. It was a play backed by preparation and training.

Both of these games serve as reminders that Hail Mary moments are not just about miracles or desperation. They require effort, foresight, and discipline. Success may not be likely, but without preparation, even a small chance is impossible. Nothing comes free. Whether in sports or in life, hard work is essential.

Back-to-School Night

October 2, 2015

Back-to-School Night is an event held at the beginning of the school year where parents meet their children's teachers and receive updates from the PTA. For me, it is also a chance to visit schools across various parts of the county. While each school runs the event a little differently, the experience is always a reminder of each school's unique character.

But a visit to one school last week reminded me, as a school board member, that there are areas where I need to be more mindful and attentive. Typically, Back-to-School Night draws large parent turnouts. School parking lots—and even surrounding streets—are often filled with cars. I usually have a reserved spot thanks to the school's courtesy, but many parents struggle to find parking.

That evening, I arrived about ten minutes before the event started, and to my surprise, the parking lot was relatively empty. Without giving it much thought, I parked and headed into the cafeteria where parents were gathering. There, too, the turnout seemed sparse. The principal assured me that parents usually arrive a bit late. While waiting, I spoke with the school's parent liaisons and learned more about the school community: about 70% of the students are Hispanic, 15% are Asian, and approximately 75% of families face economic hardship. Many parents work late into the evening, and many families do not own a car. Hearing this, I felt a deep sense of humility and regret for not having considered these realities ahead of my visit.

When it was time for me to be formally introduced to the parents and give a brief greeting, I paused to reconsider what I would normally say. In other schools, I might have shared a lighthearted story from my older child's third-grade journal—an entry written after a boy scout camp, where he humorously complained that his parents kept telling him to rest, only to follow with non-stop nagging. I had only discovered that journal after he went off to college. At the time, I thought I had been a great father, but that entry made me realize how much I had missed. I usually share that story to encourage parents to spend more quality time with their children while they are still close by.

But I could not tell that story here. A boy scout camp would feel far removed from the lives of many of these families, many of whom likely could not afford to send their children to such activities. I also could not urge them to attend games or volunteer at school. Many of these parents, I realized, might be working multiple jobs just to make ends meet.

Instead, I shared my own story—of coming to the U.S. as an immigrant 40 years ago after growing up poor in Korea. I spoke of my late mother, who worked two full-time jobs as a school and hotel custodian and cleaned homes on weekends to raise three children and send them all to college. I said that many of the parents in that room might be working just as hard as she did, but that in this country, there is still opportunity—success is possible if we work hard and stay committed to our children's education.

Fairfax County is considered one of the wealthiest areas in the United States, yet roughly 30% of students in its public schools come from low-income families.[10] That means many of them have fewer chances for enrichment experiences outside of school compared to their middle-class peers. As I continue visiting schools during Back-to-School Night season, I am reminded repeatedly of the need for thoughtful policies that help bridge this gap. It is one of the most urgent responsibilities we face.

---

10) In Fairfax County, the median income for a family of four in 2024 was approximately $155,000, ranking it fifth among all counties in the United States. Despite this, about 35% of families with students in public schools fall into the low-income category, according to 2025 statistics.

Role of Principal

November 17, 2017

Few roles in education are as critical as that of the principal. While classroom teachers are of course central to student learning, it is the principal who supports and leads the teaching staff, shaping the overall school environment.

One thing that often surprises visiting Korean educators in Fairfax County is how young many principals here are—30-something principals are not uncommon. I usually explain it this way: experience and seniority are certainly valuable, but in Korea, principals often retire not long after reaching that stage, which can be a missed opportunity to fully utilize their expertise. Over-reliance on seniority can also make one less adaptable to change or hesitant to embrace new ideas. That is why I believe in identifying promising young educators early and preparing them for school leadership roles.

This does not mean that all principals should be in their thirties. In Fairfax, most teachers retire around age 60 under the pension system, so an ideal distribution would include principals in their 30s through 50s. A mix of ages helps ensure a broader range of perspectives when principals collaborate.

Those who become principals in their thirties often follow a path that begins with just a few years of classroom teaching, during which they express early interest in administration. In

Fairfax, there is no minimum number of years required to apply for an assistant principal (AP) role. A teacher could start their career at 22, complete a master's degree in educational leadership in the evenings and during breaks over the next 2–3 years, and qualify to apply for administrative roles by their mid-twenties. Active involvement in school leadership projects during this time can strengthen their resume and interview performance. In some cases, a principal might recognize a teacher's leadership potential and encourage them to pursue this path.

Of course, applying for an AP position does not guarantee success on the first try. The interview process can take several rounds of experience to master, so candidates should be prepared to apply multiple times. For example, someone might begin applying in their fifth year of teaching and be appointed after three years—making them an assistant principal at age 30.

Once appointed, it is important not to remain at a single school for too long. Broadening one's experience across two or three schools—preferably with varied demographics—adds valuable perspective. Someone who starts in an affluent school might choose a Title I school next. Those who have only worked in predominantly white settings could benefit from experience in more diverse environments. After five to six years in different AP roles, they may be ready to apply for principal openings.

Even then, it can take multiple applications before securing a principalship. Rejection in the early rounds should be seen not as failure, but as part of the learning process. With persistence and growth, it is entirely possible to become a principal within five years of starting as an AP—and sometimes even sooner. So yes, becoming a principal in your thirties is very achievable.

Of course, not everyone will—or should—become a principal. The positions do not open frequently, and sometimes a stronger candidate may be selected. Still, for teachers interested in school leadership, I encourage early and confident pursuit of that goal—especially for Korean American teachers. Asian American educators are still underrepresented in teaching, and even more so in leadership roles like assistant principal and principal. While not every teacher must pursue an administrative path, those who are interested should not hesitate to step forward.

New Year's Day's Bows

February 23, 2024

On this past Lunar New Year's Day, I accompanied the Fairfax County Public Schools Superintendent on a visit to a Saturday Korean school. Originally, the school had asked whether I would be willing to observe some classes and take part in receiving saebae—traditional New Year's bows—from the students. On a whim, I asked the superintendent during our regularly scheduled meeting if she would like to join me. Without hesitation, she said yes. Given that she had a full day of meetings with the school board starting at 10:30 a.m. that same morning, I knew it could have been a tight commitment—but she did not let that deter her.

I had already been planning to visit the school at some point. The school rents classrooms from a public school on Saturdays, and there were some issues to be resolved between the Korean school and the host school. Thankfully, when the school reached out for help, I was able to serve as a bridge between the two parties, and a mutually acceptable solution was reached through compromise.

While I naturally feel a strong connection to Korean community issues, I am also mindful of how I represent all residents as an at-large school board member. I try to advocate while remaining neutral, especially in sensitive situations. That is why I aim to facilitate conversations rather than impose my views.

I had previously raised the Korean school's concerns with the superintendent. She likely already had some interest in visiting herself, especially since I have often emphasized the presence of numerous Korean weekend schools in the greater Washington area and the importance of fostering collaboration between them and the public school system.

Though this visit lasted only about an hour, the superintendent was visibly surprised by the size and organization of the school—280 students and twenty teachers, plus twenty assistants. More than anything, she appreciated the opportunity to experience Korean culture firsthand.

Before coming to Fairfax, the superintendent had worked in a district outside Seattle, Washington. As a white American woman, she had not had much exposure to Korean traditions. This was her first time receiving a saebae. I explained that in Korean culture, bowing to elders on Lunar New Year's Day is a traditional way to show deep respect and to start the year with grace. I also shared that students sometimes visit teachers' homes to bow, underscoring how highly teachers are regarded in Korean culture. She nodded with understanding.

We received the saebae in a hallway, seated on the floor. While I am used to sitting cross-legged, the superintendent understandably found it uncomfortable. Between groups of students, she took brief moments to stretch her legs. It was a small inconvenience, but part of the authenticity of cultural experience.

Another tradition she encountered that day was saebaetdon

(New Year's Day's gift money) and blessings bestowed. I had brought extra envelopes with money in them and handed her a few, suggesting she distribute them to the students herself. When I explained that offering a few words of encouragement after receiving bows is customary, she embraced the tradition warmly and shared kind messages with the children.

After the visit, she offered to reimburse me for the saebaetdon she had handed out, saying she felt bad about using my money. I assured her there was no need—and shared the backstory of where the money that I handed out had come from.

"About two years ago, there was a ceremony naming the gym at Thomas Jefferson High School for Science and Technology in my honor. During that event, a respected elder from the local Korean community gave me a silk pouch. Inside were fifty crisp $2 bills. She had long since retired, had no income, and was of my parents' generation. I was so touched by her gesture that I never spent the money. Instead, I kept it safely in the pouch. But this time, I opened it so that the blessings she intended for me could be passed on to the next generation."

As I told her this story, I saw something shift on her face—something heartfelt. It was, in many ways, one of the most meaningful Lunar New Year's Day mornings I have had in a long time.

Group New Year's bow: On the right, a teacher is showing the children how to perform the traditional bow.

On the far left in the back row is Mr. Han Yeon-Sung, who was the principal of the school at the time.

Time I Felt Freest

July 27, 2012

If I were to name the time in my life when I felt most at ease, without hesitation I would say it was the year I took a leave of absence from college to study Chinese in Taiwan. At the time, I was majoring in East Asian Studies with a focus on China. After graduation, I considered pursuing a degree in international relations and possibly a diplomatic career, perhaps even returning to Korea to contribute in the field of global affairs.

But as I delved deeper into my studies of China, I realized I needed a better grasp of the Chinese language. The challenge was that in the late 1970s, the United States and China had not yet normalized diplomatic relations, making mainland China off-limits. The realistic options were Hong Kong or Taiwan, and I chose Taiwan.

American universities often offer a "Junior Year Abroad" program, where students spend their junior year studying at a foreign institution, earning academic credits, and paying equivalent tuition. But that was not my case. I simply took a year off to study Chinese independently in Taiwan. There was no pressure of grades or credits.

In retrospect, I might have studied more diligently if I had had an academic goal. But that year, without deadlines or performance pressure, turned out to be one of the most meaningful experiences of my life. I could spend my time entirely as I wished. It was a precious opportunity to immerse myself in a completely new environment, meet new people, and experience a different culture. Taiwan shared some similarities with Korea as a fellow East Asian society, but I also encountered countless differences.

While there, I taught English to cover living expenses and built friendships with people my age. I rented a room in an apartment and vividly remember communicating with the landlord's family using hand gestures and a dictionary. I did my laundry by hand, experienced mild inconveniences, and delighted in discovering Taiwanese cuisine—especially the dumplings I came to love.

There were also rougher moments. I once fell ill with food poisoning and battled skin conditions. Yet even those hardships became part of a broader learning and growth process. I had the chance to observe the Korean expatriate community, and I learned about Taiwanese politics, society, and education firsthand.

Because of that experience, I have often encouraged my children to spend a year abroad as well. My older child has already graduated from college and has been working for two years, so it might be difficult now. My younger child is entering senior year of college this fall and preparing for graduate school, so taking a break may not be feasible. Still, I continue to urge both of them to explore such an opportunity.

I have suggested to my older son that he considers taking a short break before graduate school. I have also mentioned to my younger son that if he is admitted to graduate school, he might consider deferring for a year and using that time meaningfully.[11]

This idea is similar to the concept of a "gap year" before college—a period of time many American universities allow students to take after admission, offering them a chance to gain life experience and reflect on their future.

I once knew a young woman who was accepted to Harvard but decided to defer for a year. With prior approval from the university, she worked as a waitress near a ski resort in Colorado and spent her free time skiing. More than just taking a break, she read books she had long put off because of school, listened to music, and reflected deeply on herself. When she started college a year later, she was more mature and realized that the time she took was not wasted but an invaluable period of growth.

Moments of pause like this do not have to be gaps in one's life. They can be launching pads for something greater. In today's fast-paced world, I often find myself yearning for that one year in college when I lived freely and without worries.

A time when I could truly do what I wanted; when I could experience a new culture; and when I could just enjoy learning for its own sake.

If given the chance, I would love to relive that kind of freedom.

And maybe—just maybe—that day will come again.

---

11) In fact, both of my sons were born in the United States. However, the older one lived in India for a few months when he changed jobs after working at his first job for three years following college graduation. The younger one spent a semester in France during his doctoral studies and conducted research at CERN, a research institute located in Switzerland. So, both of them have had the experience of living abroad.

The Mandarin Training Center (國語中心), where I studied Chinese, was an affiliated institute of National Taiwan Normal University.

Beef noodle soup (牛肉麵): a dish I often had for lunch. For breakfast, I usually ate youtiao (fried dough sticks) and doujiang (soy milk).

Boiled dumplings: I often ate more than 30 of them in one sitting for dinner.

Artificial Intelligence

June 9, 2023

This past Monday, The Washington Post ran a feature on ChatGPT, the AI platform that has been drawing widespread attention. The article noted that, though it was only launched in November of last year, this AI tool is already performing tasks that used to be done by humans. Interestingly, just before I read the article, I had a conversation at church with my younger son—who works in AI—and some students I teach, about ChatGPT.

My first real interest in artificial intelligence began in 2016, during the five-game Go match between Lee Sedol, then one of the world's top professional players, and AlphaGo. At the time, AI was still in its early stages, and most people assumed that Lee Sedol would win. But the results surprised everyone: AlphaGo won four games to one. It was a historic moment—one in which a top human lost to an AI.

The following year, AlphaGo defeated China's Ke Jie, then the world's top-ranked player, in three straight games before "retiring" from competition, having fulfilled its purpose of demonstrating AI's capability. Since then, AI in Go has continued to evolve, and now even the current world number one, Shin Jin-Seo, is said to be two to three stones behind the best AI—roughly the difference of two or three skill ranks.

Today, professional players and hobbyists alike use AI to study Go. Matches between humans and AI are no longer relevant. Instead, AI created by humans is being used to help humans grow.

ChatGPT, for its part, can answer simple questions, generate detailed explanations, create original ideas, complete sentences, and even translate texts. But its use among students has sparked debate. Opinions differ widely on whether it is appropriate to use ChatGPT to complete assignments, essays, or research papers.

As someone preparing to return to the school board, I found this to be a particularly timely issue. So, before writing this column, I decided to try ChatGPT myself.

I first asked it to draft an article about the problems associated with using ChatGPT. Within seconds, it produced a well-structured essay. Out of curiosity, I asked again, and it generated a different version with a list of ten concerns—such as unfair advantages, hindered personal growth, plagiarism risks, lack of fact-checking, decreased learning achievement, and damaged student-teacher relationships.

Next, I asked it to write a 500-word sermon applying the biblical metaphor of "salt and light" to the Korean American community. Again, a full result appeared in seconds. Letters for immigration petitions and short congratulatory remarks for scholarship ceremonies were quickly generated in both Korean and English. I even asked it to translate one of my past columns into English, and it completed the task in under 30 seconds.

Seeing ChatGPT's capabilities made me reflect: Should we be restricting this technology? Or should we encourage students and teachers to use it actively? It has become clear to me that this is a conversation we can no longer postpone.

Using ChatGPT reminded me of the cultural shock I experienced after immigrating to the U.S. in the mid-1970s and attending high school here. Back in Korea, we were expected to do mental math or write out calculations by hand. But in American classrooms, calculators were allowed during lessons and even exams! More surprising still, the periodic table hung on the classroom wall during chemistry tests. Complex physics and chemistry formulas were provided; students were not expected to memorize them, but rather to understand how to apply them. It did not make sense to me at first, but I eventually came to see the logic and effectiveness of that system.

There is a saying: "If you cannot beat them, join them." We live in an era where we cannot stop the advancement of AI. The real question is: how should we use tools like ChatGPT? Simply banning students from using AI may not be the best solution. Instead, we should aim to help students use AI to learn more effectively, nurture creativity, and develop critical thinking skills.

To do that, we must equip them to adapt to the rapidly evolving landscape of artificial intelligence—just as I had to learn how to use a calculator decades ago. Now, we must think seriously about how tools like ChatGPT can be integrated into education.

As we enter the age of AI, it is no longer just about adopting new technology—it is about how we can use it to maximize human potential.[12]

---

12) I asked ChatGPT to help refine a piece of writing about ChatGPT itself. Here's the exchange we had:
    Me: It feels kind of funny to ask ChatGPT to edit something about ChatGPT.
    ChatGPT: I know, right? Asking ChatGPT to polish a piece about ChatGPT kind of feels like a form of "self-censorship."
    Me: But isn't this also a good example of how AI can be used as a tool to support our work? Like how calculators were unfamiliar at first but eventually became essential.
    ChatGPT: Exactly—and the key is to use ChatGPT with a critical mindset. Rather than blindly trusting it, it's important to review and refine the output—just like you're doing today!

Politics of School Superintendents

January 17, 2014

According to recent reports in the Korean media, the ruling party in South Korea is discussing ways to revise the current system for selecting superintendents of education. Since the founding of the government in 1948, South Korea's superintendent selection process began with presidential appointments; then shifted to an indirect election system with the introduction of local autonomy in 1991; and has operated under a direct election system since 2007. However, concerns are being raised about problems inherent in the direct election system.

One of the main criticisms is the excessive cost of running for office. Because of this, even highly qualified candidates often struggle to launch a campaign due to financial barriers, and concerns abound that the fundraising process opens the door to corruption and misconduct. Indeed, since the introduction of the direct election system, a number of superintendent candidates have faced investigations or trials over campaign finance issues, bribery, or improper personnel practices. There is also growing criticism that the political neutrality of education—guaranteed by the Constitution—is being undermined by overt involvement in elections by political parties, resulting in the subordination of education to political interests.

In the United States, the method of selecting school superintendents varies by state and school district. In some areas, superintendents are elected, while in others they are appointed. Typically, appointments are made by the school board, but in places like Washington, D.C., or Prince George's County, Maryland, the mayor or county executive may make the appointment. Although I do not claim to know all the systems used across the U.S., I would argue that no single method is universally superior. However, I do believe the system used in Fairfax County, Virginia—where I serve as School Board Chair—is worth considering.

In Fairfax County, the school board appoints the superintendent. By law, the initial contract term must be at least two years and no more than four years. After that, reappointments can be made for up to four years at a time, with no term limits. Meanwhile, school board members are elected through nonpartisan elections—at least on paper. Although political parties are not permitted to formally nominate candidates, they are allowed to publicly endorse them, and there are no restrictions on party involvement in campaign activities. In practice, this means these elections function similarly to partisan races, making it difficult to eliminate political influence entirely.

Since the school board election system was introduced in 1995, Fairfax County has held five board elections. In that time, not once has a candidate without official party endorsement been elected. Clearly, party backing and organized support play a significant role. Moreover, the Democratic Party has consistently held a majority on the board. Still, what is notable is that political affiliation is deliberately excluded from the superintendent selection process.

Since 1995, the county has appointed three different superintendents. During each selection process, board members reviewed candidate résumés, conducted in-depth interviews, and carried out background checks. However, they are prohibited from considering the candidate's political leanings, party affiliation, religion, race, age, or marital status. Of course, a candidate's political orientation may become apparent through background checks, but the board does not openly discuss it or use it as a criterion for selection.

For example, when Dr. Karen Garza was appointed superintendent of Fairfax County in 2013, she had previously been registered as a Republican in Texas.[13] Yet, while ten of the twelve school board members were Democrats, they did not see her political affiliation as a problem. Instead, they focused on her qualifications as an educator and her leadership capabilities as an administrator, concluding that her political background was irrelevant.

Few would argue against the importance of minimizing political interference in public education. While electing school board members inevitably introduces a degree of political influence, it is essential that voters and board members alike

---

13) At one point, I asked Dr. Garza about her political affiliation. She replied that the area where she had served as superintendent was traditionally a Republican stronghold, and that without maintaining a Republican affiliation, it would have been nearly impossible to get anything done.

remain mindful of the need for neutrality. Regardless of how the superintendent selection process is structured, one principle must remain non-negotiable: education must never be allowed to become a tool of political agendas.

Anonymous Voting

October 6, 2023

Over more than 20 years serving on the Fairfax County School Board, I have participated in countless votes on various matters. It is not unusual for board members to be split on issues—some voting yes, some no, and others abstaining. That is not a problem; in fact, it is part of the reason the board is composed of multiple members: to exchange and reflect a diversity of opinions.

But occasionally, I have also witnessed curious behaviors. Some members, to avoid casting a vote on certain issues, would quietly leave the meeting room just before the vote. Behind the boardroom is a curtained-off area where members can rest. Some would slip into that space and monitor the meeting from a screen, returning only after the vote had concluded.

By doing so, they are not marked absent but are recorded as having abstained from that particular vote. Technically, abstention is a form of expression, just like a yes or no vote. Yet these members sometimes claim they did not abstain but simply did not get to participate in the vote at all—as if to imply they made no official statement. Such avoidance behaviors are more common on controversial or sensitive issues.

Voting procedures can vary among governing bodies. While I cannot speak for every school board in the United States, in my experience, I have never seen a deliberative body composed of elected officials use anonymous voting. In a democracy, few principles are as vital as transparency for officials who were elected by the public.

The positions of elected officials are ultimately revealed through their votes in public meetings. Voters observe how their representatives vote on issues and evaluate them accordingly. For that reason, anonymous voting is practically unthinkable. There is nothing opaquer than voting without names attached.

For the Fairfax County School Board, all votes are cast publicly, regardless of the issue. Even sensitive matters like the selection of a superintendent are voted on in public. Board members express their views transparently, even at the risk of straining relations with the superintendent. That is what healthy democracy should look like.

Yes, certain matters—like personnel issues or student discipline—are discussed in closed session, as allowed by law to protect privacy. But even in these cases, the final official decisions are made in open session, and each board member's vote is clearly recorded. In student discipline cases, while federal law prohibits disclosing the student's identity, the students are informed in advance that their cases will be put to votes. As a result, they can see how each board member voted.

With that kind of transparency ingrained in my expectations, I find it odd that personnel votes in the Korean National Assembly are conducted anonymously. This includes not only past presidential impeachment votes, but also recent votes on arrest motions for opposition party leaders and no-confidence resolutions for the Prime Minister.

Some argue that anonymous voting allows for more honest expression and can lead to better outcomes. Others claim that it reflects the unique political culture of Korea. But if an elected official cannot reveal his stance transparently, can he truly be said to be fulfilling his duty as a public servant? I believe that the more sensitive and difficult an issue is, the greater the need for transparency. That is what voters expect of their representatives.

After the recent anonymous vote on the arrest motion for the opposition party leader, there was public uproar demanding to identify who had voted in favor. In such a climate, one wonders whether true voting transparency can ever take root. Still, I remain hopeful that day will come.

Funny Guy

November 2, 2010

Last week, I spent a week in Korea, having been invited to give lectures and presentations by the Seoul National University's Educational Administration Training Institute, the Korean Educational Research Association, and Korea University. I was accompanied by a senior administrator from Fairfax County Public Schools and a high school principal. At the request of the Gyeongsangnam-do Office of Education, I also visited the cities of Changwon, Masan, and Jinju for the first time.

Although I had visited Korea multiple times since immigrating to the U.S. in 1974, those visits were usually during summer break with my family. Visiting at the end of October, when the weather was perfect, was a completely new and refreshing experience. It was also the first trip to Asia for both of my companions; for the principal, it was his first international trip ever, and he even had to obtain a passport for the first time.

Despite our busy schedule, the trip was enriching, both professionally and culturally. Even before I immigrated to the U.S. when in high school, I did not have chances to travel within Korea. This visit, therefore, held special meaning for me. It was also a valuable opportunity for the Fairfax County education leaders to directly experience Korea's rapid development and strong emphasis on education.

Thanks to the invitation from the Gyeongsangnam-do Office of Education, my visit to Changwon was via Miryang. I learned that what was once farmland in the 1970s had been transformed into Korea's first planned industrial city. Its neat and well-planned appearance left a strong impression—it could stand side-by-side with any American city.

After completing all lectures, we visited Masan, home to the famous Korean lyric song "Gagopa." We saw the neighborhood where the poet Lee Eun-Sang had lived and also toured the Masan Municipal Moon Shin Art Museum, located on a hill overlooking the sea. The museum houses works by Moon Shin, a world-renowned Korean sculptor, and was originally his private museum, later donated to the city of Masan upon his passing.

In Tongyeong, we toured Dongpirang Village, known as the Montmartre of Korea, famous for its wall murals. The village, which sits on a hillside overlooking the port of Chungmu, survived demolition thanks to a community mural project. We also enjoyed the beauty of the sea off Geoje and visited the massive Samsung Shipyard, which spans 1.5 million pyeong (about 5 million square meters). In Jinju, we had the special experience of trying Jinju bibimbap, which is topped with raw beef.

We also visited Haeinsa Temple in Hapcheon, home to the Janggyeong Panjeon, which preserves the woodblocks of the Tripitaka Koreana—a UNESCO World Heritage site since 1995. We were also able to view a replica of the Tripitaka, which was listed as a UNESCO Memory of the World in 2007. Remarkably, the Janggyeong Panjeon will celebrate its 1,000th anniversary next year. That a wooden structure has remained intact for a millennium is truly astonishing.

Among all these meaningful experiences, there was also a humorous moment. I try to maintain a habit of walking early in the morning—both to save time and to get some exercise. But this early morning walk seemed a bit too much for the two educators traveling with me. When they asked, "Do we really have to walk at 6 a.m.?" I would respond, "5:30 would be even better." Each time, they were left speechless.

After our lectures and conferences wrapped up, we had a free day before flying back to the U.S. The two companions expressed interest in visiting the DMZ, but since I had been there before, I suggested they go without me. However, they soon learned that all the reservations were full. One of them emailed me:

"All the tours are fully booked. What should we do now?"

I quickly replied, clearly prepared for this moment:

"Perfect! Then let's get up and walk at 6 a.m.!"

Shortly afterward, he emailed me back—not in English, but in Korean.

"웃긴 놈."

At first, I was taken aback. But then I realized what had happened. He had likely typed "funny guy" into an online translator, and it had returned a literal Korean equivalent, which, while technically accurate, came off sounding rude or crass in Korean. A better translation would have been something like "That's funny" or "You're a character."

When I explained the translation issue to him later, his face turned pale. He had just sent what could be perceived as an impolite message to a school board member who evaluates his performance annually. He was horrified.

Thankfully, I took it in good humor, and we all had a good laugh. But the episode served as a real-world reminder of the risks of relying too heavily on machine translation—it can result in unexpected (and sometimes awkward) mistakes.

The person wearing sunglasses on the right (Dr. Peter Noonan) is the culprit. He has served as the superintendent of nearby Falls Church City since 2017 and is retiring at the end of June 2025.

Episode from a Visit to Korea

December 27, 2019

Last month, I visited Korea for about ten days with a regional assistant superintendent and a high school principal from Fairfax County, Virginia.

The assistant superintendent oversees more than thirty schools, and the principal leads a school that introduced a Korean language course for the first time this year.

Whenever I travel to Korea with educators, I emphasize two golden rules:

"We are not going to Korea to sleep."

I always explain in advance that to make the most of the short trip, we must minimize sleep time.

"Bring comfortable shoes."

Unlike in the U.S., there is a lot of walking in Korea. I try to make sure we explore as much as possible on evenings and weekends outside of our official schedule.

But when American educators try to keep up with my pace, there are often moments of rushing—and sometimes, amusing episodes unfold.

On the first weekend, we planned to visit Odusan Observatory in Paju, Gyeonggi Province. Since we could not spare a full day for a visit to Panmunjom, we decided to make a quick Sunday morning trip to the observatory instead.

From the observatory, the American educators were stunned to see North Korean land right before their eyes. The long stretches of barbed wire lining the road along the Tongil-ro highway also left a strong impression.

About 15 minutes into the drive back to Seoul:

"I lost one of my earrings!"

The assistant superintendent believed she had dropped it in the restroom at the observatory. But since we did not want to be late for Sunday church service, we could not turn back.

She said, "It is not an expensive earring, so it is okay," but there was a hint of regret in her voice. There was nothing we could do.

Two days later, we had a packed schedule in Incheon. With coats and bags moving in and out of the car all day, it was a bit chaotic. As we neared the end of the day:

"Where's my scarf?"

This time, it was quite a pricey item.

We contacted every place we had visited and the restaurant where we had lunch, but no luck. The assistant superintendent seemed increasingly disheartened. Then we opened the car trunk—just in case. We had moved bags in and out of there multiple times.

And there it was!

The scarf had been in the trunk all along. From that moment on, the assistant superintendent became the subject of good-natured teasing for the rest of the trip—for both the earring and the scarf.

After our time in Seoul and Incheon, we began our visits to other parts of country on Wednesday morning.

While checking out of the hotel, we decided to leave half our luggage behind. The principal in particular chose to wear just one suit for the trip.

But about 30 minutes after boarding the train at Seoul Station: "Oh no… I left my suit jacket in the hotel bathroom!"

The night before, he had hung the jacket there while running hot water to release the wrinkles and simply forgot it.

We could not go back, so we contacted the hotel. Thankfully, the jacket was still there, and they agreed to keep it safe until we returned.

However, the principal became anxious because we had some formal events during our visits to Yeosu, Daegu, and Busan. Luckily, just before our meeting at the Daegu City Office of Education, we found a suitable sport coat at a department store nearby. It fit perfectly, and he wore it confidently to the official event.

After our schedule in Daegu, we boarded a late-night train to Busan. As we approached the city, we began gathering our things. The principal grabbed his bag and coat.

But… he almost left the newly bought jacket on the train's coat hook by the window!

I caught it just in time and called out, startling him. He quickly retrieved the jacket.

Though the two American educators had a hard time keeping up with my whirlwind itinerary, they told me this trip would be an unforgettable memory for life.

Next time I see them, I will be sure to ask:

"Are you keeping track of your earrings, scarf, and suit jacket?"

Enjoying a break in the midst of busy schedule on Oedo Island, Geoje City, Gyeongnam

Teacher Recruitment from Korea

October 18, 2024

Fairfax County Public Schools (FCPS) in Virginia will begin recruiting teachers from Korea starting next year. The current superintendent, who took office two years ago, has decided to officially launch this initiative. Personally, this is a deeply meaningful step, as I have long had an interest in recruiting teachers of Korean heritage.

This pilot program, set to begin next year, will aim to recruit ten secondary-level math and science teachers exclusively from Korea during its first year. To lay the groundwork, I visited Korea this past August and personally shared the plan with several local education officials. I also met with education officers at the Korean Embassy in Washington, D.C., asking for help in sharing the news with the Ministry of Education in Korea and, through them, local education offices across the country. The superintendent sent an official letter to the Ministry of Education representatives at the embassy, which seems to have effectively disseminated the information throughout Korea.

Applicants must currently be employed teachers with at least two years of teaching experience—whether in public or private schools, and whether full-time or temporary. A key requirement is the ability to teach in English. Selected teachers will enter the U.S. on a J-1 visa. If family members accompany them, they will receive J-2 visas, and spouses may apply for work authorization after arrival. The visa process is handled by Participate Learning (PL), a third-party agency contracted by the school district, and generally takes about three months.

Since word of the recruitment spread, it is encouraging to hear that several candidates have already applied. The acceptance rate is known to be highly competitive—often dozens of applicants per position—and PL reportedly conducts a very rigorous review of application materials. However, so far, all Korean applicants have passed the initial paper screening, and interviews will be scheduled soon.

I was personally involved in a few aspects of the process. One applicant, for instance, listed the subject she taught in Korea as "Life Science," which caused a problem. PL's system did not recognize this as a core science subject, though in the U.S., the correct equivalent term would be "Biology." This revealed a gap in PL's understanding of the Korean education system and curriculum, an area that I hope will improve going forward.

In another case, a candidate applying with family was flagged by PL's automated system due to concerns about the high cost of living in Fairfax County. While it is understandable to request more financial information in such cases, automatically rejecting a candidate solely for that reason seemed inappropriate. I raised this issue with PL, and adjustments have since been made.

It is also encouraging that applications come from a wide

range of locations in Korea—including Seoul, Busan, Sejong, Cheongju, and Suwon. Notably, Sejong and Cheongju were not regions I visited in person, suggesting that outreach through the Korean Embassy has been effective. I want to express my appreciation to the embassy staff for their assistance.[14]

Alongside the J-1 visa program, I am also pleased to report that FCPS has decided, for the first time, to sponsor H-1B visas. These are typically reserved for highly skilled workers in fields facing labor shortages in the U.S., including teachers and IT professionals. The school system plans to hire up to ten teachers under this program in its first year. Eligible candidates must already hold a valid U.S. teaching license. In addition to math and science, the eligible positions include special education, world languages (including Korean), ESL, counseling, elementary education, school psychology, and speech-language pathology.

One major benefit of this H-1B program is that, since the employer is a local government agency (the school district), the typical lottery process is waived, and up to ten visas are guaranteed. In other words, qualified candidates do not have to worry about being randomly excluded from the program. This presents a significant opportunity for Korean nationals hoping to teach in the U.S.

I hope that the Korean American community will take full advantage of this initiative. For Korean students studying in the U.S. who are unsure about their visa status after graduation, the

---

14) After a rigorous selection process, ten teachers were chosen by the Fairfax County Public Schools and arrived in the U.S. on July 19, 2025. Their first day of classroom teaching is August 18, 2025.

H-1B program could be a crucial solution. I plan to continue working with the school district to support these efforts and look forward to strong participation and support from the Korean community.

With the ten teachers from Korea upon their arrival at Reagan National Airport on July 19, 2025. Also pictured are a staff member from Participate Learning and an official from the Korean Embassy in Washington, D.C.

Chapter 4
American Society

Introduction

It is impossible to fully describe American society in a short essay. While its modern history may not be as long as that of other nations (though that changes if one includes the history of Native Americans), the vastness of its land and the diversity of cultural and racial backgrounds among its immigrant population make it difficult to define American culture in a single phrase.

I live in Fairfax County, Virginia, a suburb of Washington, D.C., where many residents work as federal government employees or in related fields. The county is also racially and ethnically diverse.[15] I have lived in northern Virginia for all but the years I spent attending college and law school—this marks my 51st year in the U.S. But even with that, I fully recognize the limits of my experience and that it cannot be generalized to represent all of America.

Nonetheless, I can say with confidence that American society is, to a significant extent, horizontal in structure. While wealth, education, and family background may create some distinctions, they rarely serve as insurmountable barriers. This is, of course, based on my limited experience and is meant as a relative observation—especially when compared to Korea.

---

15) According to the 2024 census, the population was approximately 48% White, 11% Black, 21% Asian, and 18% Hispanic. In contrast, nationwide figures show about 58% White, 14% Black, 20% Hispanic, and just over 6% Asian.

Despite issues such as gun violence and what can seem like a high crime rate, the U.S. places strong emphasis on rule of law, legal procedures, and the protection of human rights. There is also a pronounced concern for minorities and the vulnerable. Americans tend not to hesitate in voicing their opinions, yet they also learn early on how to compromise and consider others' perspectives. Rather than focusing solely on climbing over others in competition, collaboration and communication are valued traits.

Age and gender discrimination are taken seriously, and capable individuals are recognized and rewarded. It remains a society where, by and large, effort is met with fair outcomes. There is no rigid standard or uniform goal applied to all, and the distinction between high- and low-status jobs is relatively minimal.

Of course, America is far from a perfect society. Prejudice and envy still exist, and racial tensions remain significant. Yet despite its flaws, there is much to learn from this society.

Culture Shock

September 22, 2023

Not long ago, over dinner with some former colleagues from the Fairfax County School Board, we started talking about the cultural shocks I experienced after immigrating to the U.S.

About a week after arriving, I attended school for the first time—a school in Alexandria, Virginia, that served only 9th and 10th graders.[16] I waited for the school bus near my apartment, surrounded by students who were physically bigger than I but younger in age. I had intentionally enrolled in a grade lower than I was in Korea, hoping to have more time to learn English before entering college.

Everything obviously felt unfamiliar on that first day, and I tried my best to avoid eye contact with other students. The language barrier was particularly difficult. With the limited English I had learned in Korea, I could understand only bits and pieces of what others said. In the entire school, there were only four ESL students—including me.

However, there was one student who kept trying to talk to me, despite my efforts to avoid him. I ignored him as best as I could, but he kept at it. Realizing I did not understand him well,

---

16) 9th grade in the U.S. corresponds to 3rd year of middle school in Korea, and 10th grade corresponds to 1st year of high school.

he started speaking more slowly. Then suddenly, I recognized a word—a slang term—and was shocked.

The student had asked me if I had ever had sex.[17]

I was stunned. Could someone really ask a complete stranger such a question? This kid looked no older than 13 or 14. Was this really American culture?

As my colleagues laughed at the story, I shared another episode. I said I had once been sexually harassed in high school—which immediately drew serious attention.

It happened during the summer after my 11th-grade year, when I participated in a Governor's School program. The program was held at a women's college, and female college students served as dorm proctors. Toward the end of the four-week program, I had become somewhat familiar with them, though as someone who had been in the U.S. only two years, it was still awkward talking to American women.

On the day I needed to go back home after the program all ended, as I was walking to the bus stop with my luggage to catch a Greyhound, one of the dorm proctors spotted me. She approached and gave me a goodbye hug.

Up to that point, the only woman who had ever hugged me was my mother. It was a shocking moment. That brief embrace, which must have lasted only a few seconds, felt like an eternity to me.

My fellow board members burst out laughing. They clearly found these stories of an Asian immigrant student's culture shock

---

17) The word used at that time was "screw." I was so shocked that I still remember it vividly, even after 50 years.

both entertaining and endearing. Now, having lived in the U.S. for nearly fifty years, little shocks me anymore—at least not here. But these days, I sometimes feel shocked in the opposite direction—from the news I hear about Korea.

One thing that stands out is how cases that would be treated as civil matters in the U.S. are often handled as criminal cases in Korea—things like defamation, dereliction of duty, and the spreading of false information by political candidates. In the U.S., these would typically be resolved through civil lawsuits, media scrutiny, or public criticism. But in Korea, they often lead to criminal charges. Additionally, pre-trial detention appears to be much more common in Korea. In the U.S., the threshold for detaining someone in a criminal case is quite high. In Korea, it seems detention happens more easily.

Of course, every country has its own legal system and culture. Yet, as someone who has practiced law in the U.S. for nearly four decades, I find these developments in my homeland increasingly troubling. Korea may have joined the ranks of economically advanced nations, but I find myself questioning whether its legal system and culture have kept pace.

Parenting

January 16, 2015

A few days ago, an article in a magazine caught my eye. It was written by a young Korean American attorney working at a law firm in Washington, D.C. He shared how, before starting his job at the firm, he had taken six months off to care for his young daughter at home. Some might question whether six months is truly a long time, but the message he conveyed went far beyond simply taking parental leave.

This attorney had graduated from Harvard Law School and worked as a law clerk for a year at the U.S. Supreme Court. Serving as a law clerk at the Supreme Court is considered one of the highest honors for a law school graduate—an opportunity reserved for those with the most outstanding academic records and qualifications. Ko Hong-Joo, former dean of Yale Law School and U.S. Assistant Attorney General for Human Rights, also once held that position. It was a source of pride in itself that a young Korean American had earned such a distinction.

When his daughter was born, his wife was a medical student. Without hesitation, she decided to take a year off to care for their baby—not only for their daughter's benefit but also because she wanted to fully experience motherhood. Respecting her decision, he too wanted to spend meaningful time as a father before starting his next role after the clerkship. What he feared most while watching his daughter grow was the possibility that, decades later, he might regret choosing work over family.

We often assume that men do not enjoy parenting as much as women do, but he pointed out that this is a misconception. He emphasized that for men, too, raising a child is a vital human experience.

He even cited statistics. According to a Pew Research study published in October 2013, 60% of men said that time spent caring for children was deeply meaningful, whereas only 33% said the same about their jobs. In other words, for fathers as well, parenting can be a significant source of joy in life.

He recalled that since adolescence, he had cried only twice before his daughter was born. But once his wife returned to medical school and he began taking their daughter to daycare each morning, things changed. Whenever his daughter clung to him crying, not wanting to be left behind, he felt ashamed and guilty walking away—and often cried himself. Over time, as he spent more time at home with her, his tears were no longer from guilt but from joy and emotion. Watching his daughter grow filled him with love and gratitude.

Reading this reminded me of a couple who used to live next door. Both were lawyers, but the wife gave up her career raising their two sons at home. Then one day, I noticed the husband was the one staying home. Curious, I asked him about it. He told me it was time to switch roles—he would be staying home for the next three years to care for the children and manage the household. I was surprised. I knew I could never do the same.

Another time, while organizing the house, I came across an old journal written by my eldest child when he was in sixth grade. It was from November 1999, right after I lost my bid for reelection to the school board and had been appointed to the county's planning commission. In his journal, my son had written:

"My dad is no longer a school board member. I thought I would be able to spend more time with him now, but he says he is starting a new job on a planning commission that deals with real estate development."

Reading that sentence made my heart ache. A child's early years never return. I feel deep regret and sorrow for not spending more time with them—always too busy, always thinking there would be time later. But those missed moments have left a lasting void.

Free Rider

August 18, 2017

This is a story I once heard from an acquaintance. She had immigrated to the U.S. in the 1960s and lived briefly in the South. Back then, she had to use coin laundromats because she did not have a washing machine at home. At the entrance, there were signs that read "Whites Only" and "Colored Only."

At first, she assumed these referred to white and colored clothes. It was only later did she realize that these were discriminatory signs separating white and black customers. At the time, Asians were also classified as "colored," but unaware of this, she mistakenly entered a whites-only laundromat on multiple occasions.

For a long time in the U.S., there were institutionalized forms of segregation that kept black and white Americans apart in public transportation, restrooms, restaurants, and public schools. Even interracial marriage between whites and Blacks was illegal in some states until a 1967 U.S. Supreme Court ruling. Virginia, where I live, was one of the states with such laws—meaning that Koreans could not legally marry whites, either. Though decades have passed since these laws were abolished, racial conflict still runs deep in American society.

A recent flashpoint was the violent white supremacist rally in Charlottesville, Virginia. Even more troubling was that similar groups were reportedly planning rallies elsewhere, with further clashes expected.

What shocked not only the U.S. but the world was President Trump's reaction to the events. Instead of swiftly and firmly condemning white supremacists, the KKK, and neo-Nazi groups, he gave a seemingly reluctant statement—and then held a press conference the next day reversing his position.

It has been openly discussed that Trump's base includes white supremacists. Just weeks prior, his speech at a Boy Scouts event was criticized for resembling the kind of rhetoric Hitler used with Hitler Youth. Watching these developments was chilling. Rather than leading the country toward unity, the president seemed only to be appeasing his extremist supporters.

In response to the growing "Black Lives Matter" movement, some began to chant "White Lives Matter." But the question that came to my mind was: Where are brown lives?—in other words, where do Asian Americans stand in this racial discourse?

The racial issues playing out in the U.S. are not just about black and white. These are matters that affect all who live in this country, including Korean Americans. We cannot afford to stand by quietly, treating these issues as unrelated to us.

During the 1992 L.A. riots, the conflict between black and white communities spilled over into the Korean community. At the time, some introspection revealed that Korean Americans had not done enough to participate in addressing racial issues. Over nearly 20 years of serving as an elected official, I have seen clearly that while Asian Americans are often seen as beneficiaries of civil rights advancements, they are rarely viewed as contributors to those efforts.

Some may argue that Asian Americans, having a shorter immigration history, have not had the opportunity to be more involved. But looking at our own Korean American community, there is still a noticeable lack of active engagement. While people may express concern when reading about racial issues in the news, only a small minority take part in seeking solutions.

In Washington, D.C., there has long been tension between Korean business owners and the black community. During such times, a challenging question was raised toward Korean Americans:

"Are Koreans free riding on the groundwork laid by others who fought for the American Dream?"

At the time, I felt that was unfair criticism. But watching today's racial conflicts unfold, I believe we must now commit to active participation—not just to dispel such accusations, but to fulfill our responsibility.

Racial tension remains a serious and persistent problem in America, and it is not limited to the black-white divide. We can no longer be bystanders. As part of American society, we too must take part in the solution.

The Korean American community has long been recognized as economically successful, but we still fall short in political and social engagement. Only when we speak out, participate, and stand in solidarity will we shed the label of "free riders" and be recognized as a community that truly contributes to American society.

Presidency

Year 2000
Radio AM 1310

In Fairfax County, there is a parent organization called the County Council of PTAs. This umbrella group includes the PTAs of roughly two hundred schools throughout the county. Member schools frequently exchange information and collaborate on joint projects. The organization also takes public positions on major educational issues and lobbies both the School Board and the County Board of Supervisors to secure funding for public education.

The current president of this group is Rosemary Lynch, who ran in the county's first-ever School Board election five years ago in the Lee District and lost by about one hundred votes. Her predecessor, Kenton Patti, works in fundraising consulting. During his tenure as president, Mrs. Lynch served as vice president. What is interesting is that even after stepping down, Mr. Patti continues to serve the organization in another capacity—now as the chair of an important committee.

In most cases, once someone has served multiple terms as president, he steps away from involvement. But Mr. Patti chose instead to continue serving in a different role, demonstrating what true volunteerism looked like. The presidency of the PTA Council is not an honorary title or a symbolic position; it is a role of service for the benefit of the county's students and parents. Anyone assuming the position should not treat it as a badge of honor but as a call to service—carrying out his duties faithfully to the end.

A similar example can be found in the Braddock District Democratic Committee, where I am also involved. A former long-serving chair of the committee now serves as vice chair for finance. In our Korean American community, it is hard to imagine such a scenario, but what truly matters is not the title or the position—it is the spirit of continued service. If someone is willing to serve, he should be open to any role, regardless of rank or recognition.

Even if someone has served as president, if the incoming president sees value in having that person lead a department or committee, he should be willing to step into that role with a humble heart. If more people in our community could adopt this mindset of service, our organizations would become more effective, and the Korean American community as a whole would benefit and grow stronger.

Studying Languages

September 17, 2021

After retiring from the Fairfax County School Board in late 2019, where I served for over 20 years, I began a few new volunteer activities. Among them, the most rewarding—yet also the most challenging—has been assisting with ESL classes for immigrants and teaching Korean to adult learners. I serve as a teaching assistant rather than a lead instructor, as I believe it would be irresponsible for someone like me—who has not received formal teacher training—to take on full responsibility for the class.

I immigrated to the U.S. during high school, 47 years ago. As such, I cannot claim fluency in either Korean or English. There are still many English words and expressions I do not know, and my Korean has not significantly improved since I left Korea. In fact, considering the changes in spelling and grammar since then, you could say my Korean has regressed. New slang is particularly unfamiliar. That is why I feel a responsibility to continue studying, so I do not misteach my students. I carefully review each lesson and prepare thoroughly—something that helps me grow as well. This process brings to mind several episodes from my own language-learning journey.

One such episode occurred during college. A friend studying chemical engineering at MIT was working on his senior thesis.

Like me, he had immigrated during high school. He asked me to review his thesis—not for content, which I could not understand anyway—but to check the English. The word that appeared most frequently in the paper was "balloon." Although he had spelled it correctly as "balloon," I confidently changed every instance to "baloon." He believed me and made the edits. How that paper ever passed review remains a mystery. Thankfully, he later went on to earn his Ph.D. from Caltech.

Another time, during my second year of law school, I was taking a course on criminal procedure. The local police department had invited law students to ride along on night patrols to observe police work firsthand. I was nervous about encountering a real crime, but thankfully, nothing eventful happened. At one point, the officer pulled over to draft a report. He then turned to me and asked how to spell "combative." Was it "combative" or "combatative"? I was not sure, but I did not want to admit it. As a law student, I felt I could not afford to appear uncertain over a simple word. So, I answered seemingly confidently—and got it wrong. I have never seen that officer again, which is probably for the best.

There was another incident caused by a word I did not know—again, during law school. At the end of my first year, an unfamiliar term appeared on an exam. I needed to understand it to answer the question. I could not look it up and did not want to guess. So, swallowing my pride, I approached the professor—an elderly visiting scholar from another law school and an authority on the subject. Without hesitation, he apologized for using a less common word and kindly explained its meaning. I was deeply grateful. It felt like he was covering my inadequacy with his humility.

More recently, I had a similar experience while assisting with an ESL class. We were solving a crossword puzzle together, and the clue called for a four-letter word meaning "prison." Naturally, "jail" came to mind—but the answer began with a "g." The lead teacher explained it was "gaol," the British spelling, and that it is pronounced the same as "jail." I had never encountered the word before—I did not know its meaning or pronunciation.

These experiences remind me how language learning never really ends. It demands constant effort and humility—but it is worth every step.

Father and Son McElveens

October 12, 2012

I recently attended a wedding in Charlottesville, Virginia—that of Ryan McElveen, a fellow Fairfax County School Board member. Elected with me in November of last year, he holds the distinction of being the youngest school board member in Virginia. At just 26 years old, he embodies youthful energy and determination.

His path to becoming a school board member was not without obstacles. When he first ran for an at-large seat, he sought the official endorsement of the local Democratic Party, but the number of candidates the party could support was limited. In the end, he did not receive the endorsement. He accepted this outcome with grace and expressed gratitude to his supporters before stepping aside—an act that left a strong impression on me.

Soon after, however, one of the endorsed candidates withdrew, changing the dynamics of the race. The party needed to back a replacement, and McElveen secured the endorsement by winning a vote—by just one ballot. Riding that momentum, he went on to win the general election and became the youngest school board member in the state.

The most memorable part of the wedding was the image of father and son standing together. The best man at the ceremony was an elderly gentleman with a cane—McElveen's father. I had met him before, but I did not expect to see him standing so steadfastly at his son's side throughout the event. Despite being well into his seventies and reliant on a cane, his proud presence at the wedding conveyed profound love and pride.

Mr. McElveen, the father, currently teaches English at a Fairfax County middle school. He began this second career more than ten years ago, making it a bold new start in his mid-sixties. His entry into the profession was unusual. While attending his son's middle school orchestra concert, he was approached by the principal to serve as a substitute teacher. One thing led to another, and he eventually became a full-time middle school educator.

His teaching journey actually began in 1961. He first taught at a high school, then at a women's college, and eventually served as a full professor at South Carolina State University. In 1979, during the Carter administration, he moved to Washington to work on revising terminology used in federal government documents—a role that launched his public service career. He later worked for various government agencies and public broadcasting organizations before retiring officially in 1999.

But he was not one to sit still. He found joy in teaching, especially in helping students improve their writing skills. His professional background included journalism—his first job out of college was in newspaper publishing. From 1978 for about eight years, he wrote over 800 newspaper columns. He still uses those columns as teaching tools, instilling in his students the value of good writing.

His life, however, has not been without hardships. He suffered his first heart attack in 1990 and had another last fall during a back-to-school night while meeting with parents. Fortunately, he was quickly taken to the hospital and underwent successful bypass surgery. After twelve weeks of recovery, he returned to the classroom. His doctor reportedly told him that since he was constantly active with 13- and 14-year-old students, he did not need a formal rehabilitation program.

What he emphasizes most to his students is the importance of confidence. He tells them that everyone has his own strengths, and that he must trust in himself and nurture those talents. He also shares candid advice with parents. While parental involvement is important, he has often seen how over-involvement can erode children's self-confidence. Compared to when he first started teaching in the 1960s, he observes that many modern parents are overly protective.

The image of father and son standing side by side at the wedding remains vivid in my mind. It was not just a touching family moment—it was a powerful symbol of dedication to education passed from one generation to the next. Their shared commitment to teaching left me feeling deeply grateful and inspired.[18]

---

18) Father McElveen retired in 2020 at the age of 81, and his son McElveen is currently serving alongside me as a school board member. Like me, he took a break from 2000 to 2003, so he is now in his third term. He is also a parent of two lovely daughters.

During a birthday visit to Father McElveen's classroom (2019)

Group photo from the birthday visit. Staff from the school and the school district can be seen.

Mature Split

August 3, 1999
The Washington Media

According to one statistic, more than half of married couples living in the United States experience divorce at least once. While there is no definitive data on the divorce rate among Korean Americans, it appears to be significantly high as well. As a lawyer for the past 15 years, I have worked with many Korean couples going through divorce for various reasons. Though divorce is something many wish to avoid, I have come to understand that, for those involved, the reasons can be compelling.

Yet, even after encountering more divorces than most, I find the word divorce uncomfortable. It feels like a term I instinctively want to keep at a distance. Sometimes, I cannot help but wonder if there truly was no other way for the couples involved.

Americans, by contrast, seem far less burdened by or in expressing about divorce. Of course, perhaps it is the sheer normalization of divorce—given that more than half of marriages end that way—that makes it appear unremarkable.

Not long ago, I was surprised to hear that a county supervisor I personally know pretty well had gotten divorced. Many around her were not shocked, as she had been separated from her husband for some time. While divorce itself might not have been surprising, I was taken aback because there had never been any visible sign in her demeanor or life that hinted at such a change. She was over 50, her children were grown and married, and she even had grandchildren. Her divorce at that stage in life genuinely surprised me.

But what happened after the divorce surprised me even more. A few months later, I overheard a conversation between the supervisor and her son. He was inviting her to a charity fundraiser organized by his wife's workplace—and he suggested she bring her boyfriend. It turned out she had already started seeing someone else. What stood out was the casual and open nature of the conversation. There was no sense of secrecy or embarrassment. Later, I saw her introduce this boyfriend to others in a composed and matter-of-fact way. It was hard not to notice how different this cultural response was from what I was used to.

But that was not the end of the surprises. About three weeks ago, I ran into her ex-husband at a regular meeting I attend. I assumed he had come at someone's invitation. What truly startled me was that both the supervisor and their son were also regular members of the group. I later learned it was the son who had invited his father to attend that day's meeting.

While waiting in line to register, I saw the supervisor walk in. I could not help but wonder how she would react upon seeing her ex-husband. Would she avoid eye contact? Turn away? But to my astonishment, the two greeted each other warmly. She even introduced him to others as her "ex-husband." At dinner, the divorced couple and their son sat at the same table, eating together without a hint of discomfort.

Divorce does not always arise from hatred. Even if the relationship ended in bitterness, there was once deep love between them. That should be remembered. If living together is no longer viable and divorce is the chosen path, one can still sincerely wish the other well. Particularly when children are involved, it is important to maintain at least a friendly relationship for their sake. That requires maturity and emotional generosity.

Watching the supervisor, her ex-husband, and their son engage with such grace offered me a glimpse of what a mature, dignified approach to divorce can look like.

Buying a Meal

June 25, 2021

These days, the most talked-about figure in Korean politics is likely Lee Jun-Seok, the chairman of the People Power Party. While his political philosophy and views on current issues may differ from mine, regardless of those differences, I hope he brings a fresh breeze to Korean politics—centering it more on open dialogue, robust debate, and adherence to democratic procedures. He may make mistakes due to lack of experience and still have much to learn, but I hope that people from all political sides understand this, and that Chairman Lee himself continues to grow with humility.

Last week, he met with Song Young-Gil, the chairman of the ruling party. I was curious how this meeting between a five-term lawmaker and a party leader 22 years his junior would unfold, and after reading reports of their conversation, I found both leaders deserving of praise. What stood out to me was Chairman Lee's suggestion that they share a meal together. He said to Chairman Song, "If there were a chance, I would like to treat you to a meal and, in a way, create a low-cost opportunity to learn from your political experience." Song responded with a smile, "In politics, the person currently in office pays for the meal." To which Lee quipped, "So, I propose it and still get treated."

Hearing their exchange reminded me how deeply rooted the

idea of sharing a meal is in Korean culture. Among Koreans, one of the most common greetings is "Let's grab a meal sometime." Reflecting on this cultural nuance brought back a memory from my time as a school board member, when I learned firsthand about the different norms around meals in American public life.

During my first term on the school board, The Washington Post assigned a reporter to cover the Fairfax County School Board exclusively. After our often-late-night meetings, some of us board members would go to a nearby diner for a light meal or a drink, talking casually—not about board business, of course, as it would be illegal for more than two board members to discuss school matters without public notice.

Sometimes that reporter would come to the same diner. At first, he would sit at a separate table, but eventually he would occasionally join us. Even though we were sources and he was a journalist, these informal settings made conversation more relaxed. He, like everyone else, would have a drink or two.

But he always insisted on paying for his own drinks. He never allowed a school board member or even the school district's communications staff to cover his tab. It was not much money, but he followed that principle without exception. Successive reporters also adhered to this rule. If he interviewed me over a meal, he either covered the full cost himself or, at the very least, paid for his own portion—unlike the Korean norm, where the older or higher-status person usually picks up the bill.

I recall another incident a few years ago when I had lunch at a

Korean restaurant with the Attorney General of Virginia. He was preparing for an election campaign and brought along a campaign staff. Our conversation covered not only election matters but also broader policy issues.

When I tried to pay the bill after the meal, he firmly declined. Regardless of the amount, he said, public officials should not accept meals paid for by others. In fact, since he had initiated the meeting, he insisted on paying. He also noted that his staff's meal would be covered by campaign funds. In the end, we each paid our own share.

Adapting to these American norms around meals and public service took time. Hearing that the ruling party leader in Korea told the opposition leader, "The one currently in office pays for the meal," reminded me again how important it is to understand and respect cultural differences.

Traditional Korean lunch (hanjeongsik) during the 2018 visit to Gyeongsang nam-do with the Fairfax County Superintendent. Superintendent Park Jong-Hoon and former Washington D.C. Education Center Director Kwak Bong-Jong are visible. Superintendent Park came all the way to Gimhae to join us.

Drinking with Meals

July 8, 2022

Before the pandemic, while serving as a school board member in Fairfax County, Virginia, I participated in annual trips to Korea with senior education officials from the school system. Given that Fairfax County Public Schools serves students from diverse racial and cultural backgrounds—including many Korean American students—I believed it would be valuable for educators to experience Korean culture and its education system firsthand.

During these visits, we toured local schools and met with Korean educators and education officials, gaining insights into different teaching methods and educational philosophies. Many meals were shared, and something that often felt unfamiliar to the American educators was Korea's custom of drinking alcohol with meals.

Not only at dinners but even at lunch, the host would sometimes offer alcoholic beverages. Sharing a bottle or two of low-proof beer in a relaxed atmosphere was not unusual. At first, some American educators seemed hesitant, but eventually, like the saying "When in Rome, do as the Romans do," they joined in. However, when Korean educators visited Fairfax, offering them alcohol was not easy. In the American workplace, strict rules still apply, especially regarding alcohol. I was reminded of a few episodes I experienced as a board member related to this cultural difference.

One happened years ago, during my early years on board. A board member critical of the superintendent raised an issue, claiming that the superintendent attended a school board meeting while under the influence of alcohol. The board member said that she smelled alcohol and that the superintendent's speech was slightly slurred—particularly troubling as they were seated next to each other.

The superintendent later explained that he had a glass of wine during dinner with an important guest before the meeting. He believed that it did not impair him but expressed regret that the board member had felt uncomfortable. He apologized and promised not to consume alcohol, no matter the occasion, until after official duties had ended for the day.

Another incident occurred during my time as board chair. We had a tradition of treating the school board staff to lunch once a year in appreciation for their hard work. Board members would split the cost, and after the meal, the chair would often grant the staff a half day off—a gesture they especially appreciated.

At that lunch, I ordered two bottles of wine for the group. Given the number of attendees, each person would have had only about a glass. But I noticed a subtle shift in the mood. Some staff members, despite the chair's approval, hesitated to drink, clearly still cautious about workplace alcohol policies. Some eventually took a small sip to match the tone, while others left their glasses untouched. Even though they had been officially dismissed for the afternoon, they maintained a strict stance on alcohol during work hours.

More recently, I saw this same disciplined attitude again. I invited a school official who had played a key role in the dedication ceremony in my honor for the new gym at Thomas Jefferson High School for Science and Technology to lunch, as a gesture of thanks. A large man, he was delighted when I suggested Korean BBQ. As the meal progressed, I casually asked if he would like a beer. He politely declined, saying his workday was not over yet.

So, we just enjoyed the meal with conversation. As the discussion deepened, I asked again—more gently—if he would like a beer. This time, he looked at me, smiled, and said yes. Before the drinks arrived, he pulled out his phone and requested a half-day leave from the office. He wanted to be off duty before he touched a drop. I was struck by the thoughtfulness and strict adherence with which he followed the rules. In the end, we each had two beers and finished the meal.

Seeing that, I could not help but reflect that perhaps it is this kind of principled behavior that has contributed to the strength of American institutions.

Dinner with the Fairfax County Superintendent during a visit to the Jeollanam-do Office of Education (November 1, 2018).

Mother of the Annandale Rotary Club

July 31, 2015
May 14, 2021

This past Sunday was Mother's Day in the United States. In Korea, May 8 is designated as Parents' Day to honor both mothers and fathers, while in the U.S., each parent has a separate day of celebration. This year (2021), Father's Day falls on June 20. Since my mother passed away ten years ago, I spent Korea's Parents' Day the day before, sharing a meal with my father. As usual, he had a glass of sake, and I, using driving as an excuse, opted for something lighter.

But two weeks prior, Gwen Cody, who had long been like a mother figure to me in the Annandale Rotary Club, of which I am a member, passed away at the age of ninety-nine. She certainly lived a long life. Yet, because her own mother had lived to 104, Ms. Cody had set her sights on outliving her mother. Though she fell five years short, she lived a quarter-century longer than my own mother, who passed in her mid-seventies, so I could not just feel sorrow.

Due to the pandemic, our club had suspended in-person meetings for over a year, so it had been a long time since I had last seen her. Ms. Cody made every effort to attend meetings, relying on caregivers or family if needed. She continued to drive herself into her mid-nineties. She was the club's first female president and had served as a member of the Virginia House of Delegates in the 1980s. During World War II, she worked in Paris decoding messages.

She was always cheerful, full of humor, and mingled effortlessly with people of all ages. Even past her ninety, she continued to work in real estate, guiding clients and driving several hours to visit her farm. Though she had lost her husband long ago, her sense of humor was second to none.

At nearly every club meeting, we invite a guest speaker. If the speaker happened to be a man, Ms. Cody would always ask the same question:

"Are you single, by any chance?"

"If so, I am single too, and not seeing anyone—what do you think about me?"

This always drew laughter from the crowd. Even young men old enough to be her grandsons blushed and laughed at her playful question. She insisted she did not discriminate by age and laughed it off.

Ms. Cody and I differed politically and had divergent views even on education, but during my time as a school board member, she always offered warm support. Having once held elected office herself, I imagine she empathized with and appreciated my work. From time to time, she would hand me newspaper articles or letters others had written and tell me to read them. Knowing she would ask about them the next time we met, I felt obligated to read them—at least skim them. She taught me, through her actions, the importance of listening to perspectives different from my own.

I remember her 97th birthday in April 2019. At the Rotary Club, I was usually asked to lead the birthday song for members. I knew they would ask me again. But that time, it occurred to me that I might never get another chance to sing for her. So, I did something I normally would have been too shy to do. I brought my guitar, wore a colorful party hat, and sang her a birthday song. I did not know then that it would be the last song I ever sang for her. Every Christmas party, she used to order me to perform a song, but that opportunity is now gone forever.

When my father occasionally says he is not feeling well or wonders aloud if he has lived long enough, I always tell him about Ms. Cody, who remained so active well into her nineties. But now, I can no longer point to her as an example. That is why, even during dinner with my father last Saturday, I could not bring myself to tell him that Ms. Cody had passed away.

It wasn't winter, but I sang Lee Jong-Yong's 'Winter Child.'

Chapter 5
Relationship with Father

Introduction

Just before writing this, I attended a high school production of the musical Big Fish.[19] It is a story that traces the bond among three generations—a grandfather, a father, and a son. What struck me most in the musical was a song titled "Stranger." If I were to translate that title into Korean, I would choose the word "낯선 자."

The song features a newly married man, preparing for the birth of his first child, reflecting on his relationship with his own father. He recalls the many stories his father used to tell when he was young—tales that painted the father as a kind of hero. And yet, he always harbored doubts: Were those stories really true? Did such things actually happen? Were they perhaps exaggerated? Even now, thirty years later, he confesses that his father still feels like a stranger. But then, he adds, that stranger is also someone he has long known deeply.

As I listened to the song, I could not help but think of the many stories my own father used to tell me. Some of them, too, cast him in a heroic light. He told those stories repeatedly, for decades, until the end of his life. When the same stories came up, I would sometimes listen with only half an ear. At other

---

19) This musical features music and lyrics by Andrew Lippa and is based on Daniel Wallace's 1998 novel, as well as the 2003 film written by John August and directed by Tim Burton. Its premiere performance took place in April 2013.

times, I would try to stop him, saying I had heard them all before. Deep down, I probably questioned whether they had been embellished—or whether they had really happened at all.

Now, I find myself realizing that I, too, told many stories to my two grown sons as they were growing up. Listening to "Stranger," I began to wonder how my sons have taken in the stories I have shared. Have they, perhaps, ever seen me as a stranger too? Someone they thought they knew well simply because I was always around—but who still, somehow, felt unfamiliar?

They say that people truly grow up only after their parents pass away. I was not unaware of that notion, and yet, it was not until I had lost both of mine that I began to truly come to terms with it.

Father

March 23, 2011

Compared to the fathers of my peers, my father is relatively young. During the Korean War, he fled south alone during the January 4th retreat, and perhaps because he longed for family, he married at a young age. When I was a child, I sometimes felt embarrassed that my father was younger than those of my friends. But as I have grown older, I have come to realize how fortunate it is to have a young father. The wish that our parents will be with us as long as possible—and in good health—is a universal hope among children.

My father retired more than ten years ago. These days, his favorite activity is line dancing. Unlike me, he is naturally flexible and has a great sense of rhythm—he moves through the steps with ease. When he was younger, he was good at ballroom dancing and even taught his friends. His passion for line dancing is remarkable. He sometimes sits in front of the computer for hours watching instructional videos and mastering new steps. As his son, I am grateful that he enjoys his free time with a hobby he loves. It also helps him stay physically active, so I often recommend it to others.

My father is also quite handy—another trait I unfortunately did not inherit. Whenever something in the house needs repair, he becomes the handyman who takes care of it. From electrical or plumbing issues to broken furniture, he fixes them all himself. I sense that, even after retirement, he takes quiet pride in still being able to help his son. Sometimes I intentionally ask him for help just so he can feel that sense of usefulness. He also has a keen eye—while I struggle with assembly instructions, he can look at a picture of the finished product and put it together in no time.

Recently, my father called to say he had not been feeling well. He had not been eating properly for nearly two weeks. He lives just five minutes from my house, and though I had visited him a few times during that period, he had not said a word about how he was feeling. It turned out he had been skipping meals the whole time. When I asked in frustration, "If you were feeling unwell, you should have gone to the doctor right away," he simply said, "I thought it would pass." He has always been reluctant to visit hospitals, but I was stunned that he had just endured it quietly.

Since it was the weekend, I waited until Monday and immediately scheduled a gastroscopy. But what worried him most was not his health. He had been caring for my mother, whose mobility had been declining for several years. His greatest concern was: if he had to undergo surgery, who would take care of her?

My father had always been healthy and taken good care of my mother, so I had never given the matter much thought. But this incident brought reality home. If she had to move to a nursing home, would there be a facility with space? What would the cost be? Questions I had never prepared for suddenly flooded my mind. I had watched friends with aging parents deal with these issues, but I never imagined they would arrive so suddenly in my own life.

I told my father we would think about all that only after seeing the results of the endoscopy, but in my heart, I felt an urgent need to prepare. I started thinking about whether we could hire a caregiver, and what Medicare or health insurance might cover.

Fortunately, the test results showed nothing serious. Surgery was not necessary, and medication would be enough. The immediate concerns we had been facing were eased for now, but I was reminded once again of my parents' aging and realized how unprepared I had been.

Even though I have seen others lose their parents, I had not truly reflected on what that might mean for myself. Now I see that I cannot afford to keep putting it off—that is the sad truth.

Until now, even the idea of where my parents would be buried after they passed seemed too taboo to bring up. But through this recent experience, I learned for the first time that my parents had already prepared their burial sites long ago.

I feel deep sadness. Can they not just stay with us for a long time? Why must we all eventually face farewell?

Dad trying to pull out a wooden block from the very bottom during a Jenga game (April 21, 2021).

My father and I teamed up and ended up in a match against a pair of American sisters we met by chance.

Father's Counterattack

December 25, 2020
December 11, 2020

My father is still young. During the Korean War, he fled to south alone from his hometown in North Korea. Perhaps because of the loneliness of living without family, he married early. That is why there is only a 24-year age gap between us—we were even born under the same zodiac signs. Still, at 87 this year, he is undeniably getting on in years. He is stubborn and proud, and in that respect, I take after him exactly. When two men with such similar personalities get into an argument, it is quite a scene. Of course, from my perspective, he is being unreasonable, while I am only trying to rescue him from logical fallacies out of filial devotion—or so I like to think.

Before the pandemic, I regularly got together with my father, who lives not far from me, for meals. He enjoyed our time together, sipping soju and retelling old stories. He also loved exploring new restaurants—even if they did not serve soju, he was curious as long as it was a new place. But in those conversations, I sometimes pointed out logical inconsistencies in his claims, which would often escalate into debates.

To support his points, my father frequently cited internet search results. I would rebut, insisting that he should double-check his sources. Many of our debates ended without resolution.

But my father never let it rest. He would go home, dig up more information online, and come back at our next meeting with counterarguments and evidence—especially targeting the points I had challenged. Since I did not research as thoroughly as he does, I was often caught off guard. In those moments, my final line of defense was, "Not everything you read on the internet is true." He would then dismiss that as a weak argument, and I would retort that he was being unreasonable. And so, the stalemate would continue.

Then one day, he got into a car accident. While turning left out of a parking lot onto a main road, he collided with a car going straight. When I arrived at the scene, I saw that making a left turn there required crossing double yellow lines. I told him, "You are not supposed to turn left here. Even if it is inconvenient, you need to turn right and go around." He replied, "I did not realize that." It was a basic traffic rule every driver should know, but I did not press him further.

I picked him up and brought him to my office to contact the insurance company. While arranging for his car to be towed, I asked what to do with the keys. At first, the insurance rep said they were not needed but then called back to ask us to leave them in the car. So, we had to go back to the vehicle.

On the way, I suddenly remembered a shortcut. But to take it, I had to make a left turn. I stopped, signaled, and waited for traffic to pass. That is when my father, watching the road closely, said in a quiet but confident voice,

"Is it not illegal to turn left here, since you have to cross double yellow lines?"

Aha! Even in this situation, he was not going to miss a chance to counterattack. His quick wit was anything but that of an 87-year-old man. And what was my response as the son being countered? I firmly replied, "Of course it is illegal," —then made the left turn anyway.

I wrote about this exchange in a newspaper column I contribute to regularly. I was certain my father, once he read it, would find yet another point to argue. And when he did, we would open a bottle of soju—something we had not done since the pandemic began—and go another round. But honestly, I am just grateful that he is still sharp enough to challenge me. That is the father I remember—still spirited and full of life.

A few days after the column was published, I saw him again. By then, his car had been declared total, and we needed to retrieve his belongings from it. As he got into my car, he suddenly handed me an envelope. It looked like he had withdrawn some cash from the bank.

"We have not had a meal together in a while. Go and have a nice one," he said.

Ah! He must have heard about the column from someone. I did not know how to respond. I resisted the urge to open the envelope immediately and waited until I had dropped him off at home. As he walked inside, I carefully opened it. Inside there were ten crisp $100 bills. "I cannot eat that much in one meal..." I thought. I had expected maybe $100 in small bills, not this. He is not wealthy—he lives on Social Security and a modest pension. It was a big counterattack.

A few days later, we went to look at cars together. Debating whether to buy new or used, he said that since he would not be driving much longer and rarely used the car anyway, buying new would be a waste. From my point of view, this could be his last car, so I thought a new one might be better. But since I was not paying for it, I could not insist.

That day, he test-drove a car and said he would think it over. On the way home, he said,

"Son, is your office running all right these days? I cannot take money with me when I die. Should I give you ten grand?"

Oh, this old man—he drives me crazy! He hesitated over buying a new car because it would be wasteful, yet he was ready to give money to his nearly 60-year-old son without a second thought. And it is not like he even has a fortune to take with him. Things are not quite like they were before the pandemic, but I assured him the office was doing okay—and my heart swelled.

I had expected him to respond to my column with another verbal counterstrike. But instead, he countered with dinner money and concern for my work. My father is a master of the counterattack. I wonder how I might answer his latest move.

As we close out the long and difficult year of 2020, my father gave me an incredible gift. I am grateful. In the end, he decided on a used car.

Sending Off Father

February 17, 2023

My father is gone. He has gone to join my mother, who passed away about twelve years ago. Having lived nearly 90 years, one could say he lived a long life. But for me, who had believed he would easily reach one hundred, it was a shock.

Last weekend, three weeks after his passing, we held his funeral. Because he died far away, it took some time to bring his body here. Following his wishes, the funeral was held privately, with only family in attendance. Considering he lived in this area for 50 years and surely had many acquaintances, I felt sorry for not notifying others and allowing them to say goodbye. But knowing my father's personality—how he disliked causing inconvenience to family and friends—this too felt like a choice true to who he was.

Everyone has a unique personality, but my father's was especially distinctive. As much as he disliked change, he had incredible patience. Until the day he died, he had ramen for breakfast almost every single morning. No matter how often I told him it was not good for his health, it made no difference. He would say, "If it were really that bad, how could I have lived this long?" —a response that was hard to argue with. I was somewhat relieved when, at some point, he began using less than half the seasoning packet to reduce his sodium intake.

After immigrating to the U.S. for work, my father stayed with the same employer until retirement. Since his English did not improve much, he never sought promotion, but he took immense pride in his skills repairing electric motors. He often boasted that he had personally fixed many of the HVAC systems in federal buildings in Washington, D.C. The story of how he came to the U.S. a year before our family and threatened to quit the job due to its low wages—resulting in a dramatic pay raise—was one he never tired of telling, and I never tired of hearing.

For decades, his lunch at work was always a bologna sandwich. The menu never changed. How he managed to eat the same thing for so long without getting sick of it remains a mystery. After dinner, his only hobby was playing solitaire poker for hours at the dining table—every day, without fail.

It was unexpected when he moved into a nursing home with an adult daycare facility but could not adjust and soon left. He stayed at my house for a few weeks before we all decided it made the most sense for him to live with my sister, the only one of his three children who was retired and could care for him full-time. At first, everything went smoothly. But about a week later, I received news that his condition had suddenly worsened.

I quickly booked a flight and rushed to be by his side the next day. After a long journey of more than ten hours, I found him much thinner. My brother-in-law and I helped him to the table and poured him some soju, his favorite. I joined him for a couple of drinks. A little while later, he went to bed. I lay beside him, holding his hand. Though his body had grown thin, I could still feel the firmness of his bones. I told my sister and her husband to go home and get a good night's sleep for once—I would stay with him that night.

I spent the night at his side, and the next evening flew back home due to prior commitments I was not able to get out of. After taking care of a few things and sleeping one more night, I received a message from my sister early in the morning.

"Dad is gone."

Just like that, after a deep sleep lasting 55 hours.

The first person who came to mind after reading the message was my second son in New York. My first son in Boston could not travel due to his newborn, but the second son had planned to fly out that morning to visit his grandfather. I called him right away, only to learn he had already heard the news from his aunt. Without even canceling his flight, he was on a train heading down—just wanting to be with me.

A wave of sorrow over my father's passing, mixed with deep gratitude for my thoughtful son, swept over me. My eyes filled with tears.

A few days before leaving for my eldest sister's home in Hawaii, singing together at my house on Lunar New Year's Day in 2023.

Having a glass of beer (July 23, 2022). Used as a memorial portrait.

Words I Never Said to My Father

June 14, 2024

This Sunday is Father's Day in the United States. Although it may not be celebrated as widely as Mother's Day, flower shops still get crowded, and restaurants bustle with family gatherings. I, too, have two grown sons and have now become a grandfather. So, perhaps I deserve a bit of appreciation on Father's Day. But still, every year when this day comes around, it is my own father who comes to mind before I think of myself.

Since my father passed away early last year, this marks the second Father's Day without him. The realization that I no longer have a father to honor weighs heavily on me.

Before he passed, my father decided to move to Hawaii, where my younger sister lived. His health had declined rapidly, and among his three children, she was the only one retired and in a position to care for him. It was the most practical choice. Still, leaving the community he had called home for nearly 50 years to move somewhere unfamiliar was not easy. As his eldest child, I also struggled to accept it. But I could not offer him the same level of care that my sister could, so I had no choice but to come to terms with it.

A few months before his departure, my father's condition

worsened, and he spent most of his time in bed. My younger son, who lives in New York, and my sister's son, his grandson from California, visited to say what might be their final goodbyes. The two of them sat quietly by his side, listening to his soft-spoken words, holding his frail hands, and thanking him for all he had given them.

Watching them, I thought they did well. But I myself could not bring myself to say the same. Even as my father said he would recover in Hawaii and return to Virginia to live past a hundred, I knew that was unlikely. Though I feared we might never meet again, I could not say anything that sounded like a farewell. I did not want to. Admitting that possibility felt too painful.

At just seventeen, my father had fled to south during the Korean War, leaving behind his widowed mother and two younger brothers in Haeju, North Korea. He lived a difficult life. And yet, he sacrificed so much for his children and family, supporting me unstintingly even during tough financial times. Still, I could not thank him in that moment. I tucked those words away deep inside, telling myself I would say them after he got better and came home.

There was something else I never said. I wanted to ask if he would not like to see his newborn great-granddaughter—my one-month-old granddaughter—before flying to Hawaii. The baby was too young to travel far, so I thought perhaps he could meet her once before he left. I wanted to tell him that she had the right to be held by her great-grandfather, and that such a moment should be captured in a photo. But I could not say that, either. I worried it would sound as though his trip to Hawaii was going to be his final journey. And I did not want him—or myself—to face that truth.

My father eventually left for Hawaii. Just two weeks later, he left on an even farther journey. I truly did not expect him to pass so soon. That was when I truly understood the truth—that no one ever knows when someone's final journey will come.

Now, as another Father's Day approaches, I still wonder whether I was right not to say the things I held back. Should I have had the courage to speak, or was it better that I stayed silent?

One thing I know for sure: if he were still alive, we would have shared a bottle of warm sake over his favorite sashimi and sushi. The ache of not being able to do that this year is strong.

And if I had just one more chance to see him again, there is something I would say—something I never once said aloud in his lifetime:

"Dad, I love you."

Life

December 23, 2022

Another year is coming to a close.

Even for those who are not Christians, this time of year brings anticipation—with Christmas Eve tomorrow and Christmas the day after. For Christians, no moment of life's arrival is more significant than the birth of Jesus. The appearance of that small life in a manger became the foundation of a faith that believes that that small life lies not only at the center of the past two thousand years, but of all human history.

I have never thought so deeply about the meaning of a single life as I have lately. Last weekend, I met my first grandchild. Only a week old, she was too young to travel, so I had to go to her. Though I was only able to stay a single night, I was reminded that nothing is more precious than the excitement and hope a new life brings.

I marveled at how such a small being could exist and reflected once again on how much love and care a helpless life needs before she can stand on her own. And I realized that every person around us has gone through that same journey to become who they are today. In the end, we are all beings nurtured by someone's love and care. That thought led me to resolve to treat those around me with more sincerity in the new year.

Yet even amid these thoughts about life, a quiet sorrow has crept in—concern for my father's health. I always believed he was healthier than anyone, but seeing him suddenly grow frail has made me realize just how unprepared I am to say goodbye. My experience of losing my mother over ten years ago was not enough to brace me for this. And it pains me to know there is not much I can do for him.

Not long ago, my sister—who came from afar to care for him—told me my father had said something like this:

"In my younger years, I had a reason to live because I had to provide for my family. And as I got older, I found meaning in helping others because I was still healthy. But now, I have no one left to be responsible for, and without my health, I can no longer help anyone. Most of my old friends are already gone. Life no longer has meaning."

I wondered how I would have responded if I had heard those words from him directly.

The topic of "life's meaning" is one I have also been contemplating lately. This year, I received my Medicare card—my official entry into the category of "senior citizen" in America. I have started thinking seriously about when the right time to retire might be, and how best to spend the time that remains after retirement.

Not long ago, at a public event, I spoke about the three "T"s we are all given: Treasure, Talent, and Time. I do not have much to boast of when it comes to treasure. But if I do possess a unique talent, how can I use it in the best and meaningful way? And while I do not know how much time I have left, how can I spend it wisely, with the greatest purpose?

Since retiring in late 2019 from 25 years of concurrent public service, I have reflected on how I have used my time and abilities over these past three years. Of course, the pandemic brought unusual circumstances, but still—was I truly satisfied with how I spent those years? And how should I live from now on to have no regrets?

Last weekend, I gazed quietly at my newborn grandchild and asked myself:

"What kinds of stories will I be able to tell her as she grows up?"

And one day, when I leave this world, what kind of grandfather will she remember me as? What kind of life will I have lived which she can hold onto?

As I am preparing to greet the new year, I hope to find an answer to that question.

Chapter 6
Relationship with Children

Introduction

There may be no topic as inexhaustible as that of one's children. It feels like a lifetime of love is still not enough, and yet, children can also make us angry. When they do well, we praise them lavishly, but at the slightest misstep, we may feel disappointed. No matter how well they do, most parents cannot help but wonder, "Could they have done even better?" We want our children to have everything we did not, while at the same time placing expectations on them we could not meet ourselves. And then we justify it with that all-too-familiar line: "It is all for your own good."

While we may intellectually understand that parents and children can see things from completely different perspectives, our hearts do not always follow that logic—leading to conflict. We may believe we are treating all our children equally, but from their point of view, it does not always seem that way. And when children do not acknowledge or reciprocate all we have done for them, it may sting.

There are times when I wonder how much advice is appropriate, and where the line is between helpful guidance and nagging. But simply standing by and saying nothing feel like neglect. After all, what parent can raise a child without saying a word?

My two sons were born in the United States and are now in their mid-to-late thirties. My older son is married and made me a grandfather two and a half years ago. But my younger son is not married yet, and though I try not to dwell on it, I cannot help but worry. Still, I know that saying the wrong thing might only backfire, so I bite my tongue again and again. My own parents did not nag me much when I was growing up, and I should follow their example—but the habits of a lawyer who made a living with words for forty years are hard to break.

Yet, I can say with confidence that I never forced my children into any particular path. I respected their choices and supported them wholeheartedly. Well—now that I think about it, I should revise that last sentence slightly. I did tell them, if possible, not to become doctors. That is because I saw too many smart Asian students aiming for medical schools, and I encouraged my sons to explore other fields. On that point, I have no regrets.

Between Father and Son

June 16, 2011

Last weekend's band concert at Lake Braddock Secondary School in Fairfax County left a deep impression on me in many ways. As a school board member, I have been invited to many school concerts over the years, but this particular performance was especially meaningful. It marked the retirement of Mr. Roy Holder, who had conducted the school band for the past twenty years and was now leaving to become president of the National Band Association. The concert served as a special farewell to his long career.

The 750-seat auditorium was not only filled to capacity, but extra chairs had to be brought in to accommodate the overflow audience. The highlight of the evening was Tchaikovsky's 1812 Overture, performed by a combined group of about 150 alumni and 185 current student band members. The emotion of that moment was indescribable. The cannon blasts and ringing bells in the final movement felt like a powerful reenactment of the Russian victory over what was thought to be the invincible French army in the War of 1812.

But what left an equally lasting impression on me that night was not just the grand finale. It was a quiet, personal moment—when one graduating student performed a trumpet duet of

Tennessee Waltz with his father. After the student completed his solo and remained standing at center stage, his father, who had long volunteered with the school band, was specially invited on stage. As he walked over, he gently bumped his clenched fist against his son's, and the son responded by putting his arm around his father's shoulder. It looked less like a father-son moment and more like two long-time friends sharing the stage. Their duet felt sweeter than the song itself.

Watching them, I found myself wondering: What could I share with my father in a moment like that?

My relationship with my father is not bad, but it has not always been smooth, either. Like many parents of his generation, he was not comfortable expressing affection. Having lost his father early and raised by a single mother, he fled to south alone as a teenager during the Korean War. Overcoming countless hardships shaped his stubborn and resolute character, and I struggled to adjust to his way of expressing himself.

Whether in Korea or in the U.S., I rarely had heart-to-heart conversations or shared experiences with my father. And as life got busier, my time with him dwindled. As a child, I remember playing baduk (go) or janggi (Korean chess) with him on occasion, but it has been nearly 40 years since we last played. After the concert, I called him early Sunday morning and asked if he would like to go for a walk together. As expected, he responded with his usual gruffness.

That made me wonder: What can I, as a father, share with my sons?

When they were young, we would play soccer, basketball,

and card games. But as time passed, I felt those shared moments becoming fewer. Sometimes, when I try to start a conversation, I get the sense they just want to end it quickly. Maybe it is just a phase—they are in their early twenties, trying to be independent and seeking distance from their parents.

One day, I was walking upstairs from the basement when my older son happened to follow behind. Suddenly, with a mischievous grin, he jabbed me playfully in the backside with his fingers. It was such a small, silly act, but it warmed my heart more than I could explain. I almost wanted to say, "Do that more often." I wished we could go back to being playful and relaxed, like good friends.

And then I wondered: Could my own father be quietly waiting for a playful moment like that from me? Maybe he, too, shares the same longing but just does not know how to express it. Have I been ignoring that unspoken wish?

So now I am seriously considering this: the next time I see my father, maybe I should do what my son did. Sneak behind him and poke him playfully in the backside with two fingers. What would his reaction be? It sounds ridiculous, but I find myself genuinely curious—and perhaps a little excited. I imagine the surprise on my father's face if his fifty-something-year-old son pulled such a childish stunt. It might just be the lighthearted moment we both need.

Three generations of men just before a crab feast in St. Michaels, Maryland (September 18, 2016).

When Children Make Mistakes

October 15, 2021

A few days ago, I went to the pharmacy inside a local supermarket to get my COVID-19 booster shot. Though I had made an appointment in advance, there was still a short wait. The waiting area was filled with people of all ages, many there not just for COVID shots, but also for flu vaccinations.

Across from me sat a white father, probably in his 40s, with his three young daughters. He was chatting with his eldest daughter, who seemed to be preparing to get her driver's license. Their conversation soon turned to a time they had lived in Japan.

At that moment, the daughter glanced at me and quietly whispered something to her father—perhaps because she noticed I was Asian.

The father suddenly seemed cautious with his words, which made the situation feel more awkward than necessary.

"I am not Japanese... and it was not even a bad story..." I thought.

His excessive caution actually made me more uncomfortable. So, in an effort to lighten the mood, I started a conversation.

"Is your daughter getting ready to take her driving test? Congratulations! It reminds me of when my kids got their licenses back in high school. Parents still have to help with about 40 hours of practice driving, right?"

The father nodded and replied, "Yes, that is right."

"I used to take my kids to the high school parking lot early Saturday mornings to practice. I had them start with backing up—definitely not easy at first. How is your daughter doing with parallel parking?"

He laughed and said, "We have not gotten that far yet."

"Oh, that is normal. But you know, once they get their license, the insurance premiums go way up. I was shocked at how much ours increased. But do you want to hear something funnier? A few years ago, my second son, who was in grad school at the time, was still on my policy. At some point, during a renewal, my premium ended up being higher than his! In other words, the insurance company decided that I was more likely to get into an accident than he was. That was... humbling. But I tried to act unfazed. Ha!"

The father chuckled in agreement. The atmosphere seemed to relax.

I continued.

"Do you know where my oldest had his very first accident, not long after getting his license?"

"Where?"

"Believe it or not—our own driveway!"

The father looked surprised.

"Hard to believe, right? It was just a few days after he got his license. One evening, he said he was going out for a quick drive. I told him to be careful. But not long after he left, he came right back. I asked, 'Back already?' He hesitated and said, 'Dad... I scratched mom's car while backing up.' And it was a brand-new car too!"

"Honestly, I could not help but laugh instead of getting angry. I mean, how far could he have reversed to mess that up? But when I saw how pale he looked, I knew he was really worried. So, I comforted him. I said, 'It is okay. Everyone makes mistakes. It is not like you did it on purpose. No one got hurt, and the damage is not that bad. We can fix the car. Do not worry too much. I had an accident not long after I got my license, too.' That seemed to calm him down."

I looked at the father and added,

"There is really no need to scold kids over mistakes they have already made. Imagine how upset they must be themselves. As parents, we do not need to make it worse by piling on guilt over something they cannot undo. Whether it is an accident, falling behind in school, or making a bad choice, if they already understand their mistake, I think it is better to offer comfort and encouragement than criticism. Of course, I am not saying we should let everything slide. But I do believe that yelling or punishment is not always the wisest or most effective response."

The father listened quietly and then nodded.

"I really agree with that. I am going to try that approach with my daughters."

I smiled and said,

"Hope I did not sound like some preachy old guy giving unsolicited advice."

He laughed, too.

"No, thank you. That was a great story."

And with that, the awkwardness from earlier completely disappeared.

If we run into each other again someday, maybe next time, he will be the one to greet this old-timer first. Ha!

Conversation with My Younger Son

January 22, 2021

I have two sons in their early thirties. The older one lives in the Northeast, and the younger one in the Pacific Northwest. The two brothers share many similarities, yet they are distinctly different in some ways. Unlike the always composed older one, the younger often strikes me as someone who might need a bit more looking after. At the same time, he is warm and affectionate—he calls us about once a week to check in and chat about daily life. Thanks to him, I get occasional glimpses into the thinking of today's younger generation.

He completed college in the Northeast and earned his graduate degree in the Midwest, but he was determined to find a job in the Pacific Northwest. He had already ruled out a future in academia during graduate school but still wanted to live in the Pacific Northwest for a few years—a region young professionals often find appealing. Perhaps it was due to what he had heard from his brother and high school friends who had worked there. Even the only internship he pursued during graduate school was in that area, and ultimately, the same company offered him a job after graduation. He seemed to have liked the work environment and conditions.

However, not even a year into the job, he decided to switch. It was not that he was dissatisfied with his first position, but the new opportunity was more closely aligned with his graduate research. The first company was relatively small, while the new one was a global corporation. He wanted to gain experience there—and the compensation was better. Although I worried that he did not stay long at his first job, his reasoning for the move made sense, and I did not object.

But less than a year into his second job, he was once again considering another move. As a result, whenever he called, I asked him about the reasons and progress, offering my thoughts in return. His main motivation this time was his desire to return to the East Coast, where both his parents and brother lived. I had no reason to oppose the idea—on the contrary, I welcomed it wholeheartedly. Truth be told, I secretly wished he would move to the Washington, D.C. area, but knowing that was probably too much to ask, even just New York would be wonderful.

Yet, there were clear differences of opinion between us. While I was not the one finding him jobs or responsible for his future, I owed him some fatherly advice. I suggested that instead of changing companies again, he consider transferring to a New York-based team within his current company. Experience at a major firm carries weight anywhere, and although I understood the restlessness often seen in the younger generation, I cautioned that frequent job-hopping might not sit well with future employers. I asked him to consider how he would feel, if he were the hiring manager, reviewing a candidate who changed jobs every year—would he feel confident about that candidate's long-term commitment?

He said he understood my point but also offered logical reasons for his own thinking. He assured me he was taking my concerns into account. As the conversation wound in circles, I eventually said, "We do not have to decide today."

His response was sharp.

"It is not 'we.'"

"'I' do not have to decide today."

He was reminding me that the decision was his alone—not a joint one between father and son. In that moment, I realized my misstep. That was not what I had meant—but it had come out that way.

On the Brooklyn Bridge (December 24, 2023)

A photo taken in Long Island City with Manhattan in the background (July 1, 2023). The Empire State Building is visible on the left in the distance, and the Chrysler Building can be seen on the right.

Ring Story

February 5, 2021

Last week, my older son who lives in the Northeast sent me a photo—a close-up of his hand wearing a wedding ring.

The wedding had originally been planned for the previous summer, but due to the pandemic, it was postponed for a year. Then, earlier this year, they decided to cancel the rescheduled wedding altogether and instead simply register their marriage. A few weeks later, they bought their rings, and he sent me the photo after trying his on. They had not officially registered yet, but he said they would need the rings anyway, so they got them early. He added that although he had not worn it outside, it felt strangely significant just wearing it around the house.

That photo reminded me of a question my son had asked several years ago. While filling out a graduate school scholarship application, he asked whether the engagement ring he had bought for his girlfriend should be counted as an asset.

At the time, he had worked for a few years after college and had decided to pursue graduate studies. Before starting school, he planned to propose, and so he bought a ring. He and his girlfriend had first met in their freshman year of college, dating for about a year before parting ways. After graduation, they reunited, and by then had known each other for almost a decade.

Before proposing, he thought it was important to first get

permission from her parents. He had heard that it was a cultural custom in her country. However, since he wanted the proposal to be a surprise, he had to contact her parents secretly.

After much effort, he managed to speak with her father, who lived on the other side of the globe. But her father said, "This is not the kind of conversation to be had over the phone. You should come and speak with me face to face."

Caught off guard, my son was not sure what to do.

To visit her parents without her knowing would require at least three days: one for the flight there, one for the visit, and one to return. He would also have to use some of his savings—set aside for tuition and living expenses—to cover the travel. But he could not see any other way around. He decided to tell his girlfriend that he had a business trip and began looking into flights.

Not long after, her father called again.

"If you are coming, do not come alone. Bring my daughter with you."

Oh no!

That would, of course, completely ruin the surprise proposal. My son was caught in a dilemma—he could not very well defy her father's request, but he also could not proceed with his original plan. In the end, he decided to delay the proposal. First, he would find a natural opportunity for the two of them to visit her parents together, and then wait for the right moment to ask. He hid the ring in a safe place so she would not find it.

Fortunately, she never discovered the ring. But when he was filling out the graduate school financial aid application, he hesitated: Should I list the ring as an asset?

That was the question he had asked me.

To this day, I am still not sure whether he was joking or serious. On the one hand, the ring was something he had bought with his own money, and technically a valuable item—so it could be considered an asset. But on the other hand, since he planned to give it away, maybe it did not count. I do not remember giving him a clear answer. I think I just laughed and moved on.

Hearing last week that he now had his wedding ring made me think, "He has really grown up." My heart swelled with pride.

And yet, I was also tempted to say, "When I was your age, you were already two years old." But I bit my tongue. I remembered the advice of more experienced parents: sometimes, saying too much can backfire.

Still, I can't help but hope that if they plan on starting a family, they will consider the age-old wisdom of having children while still young.

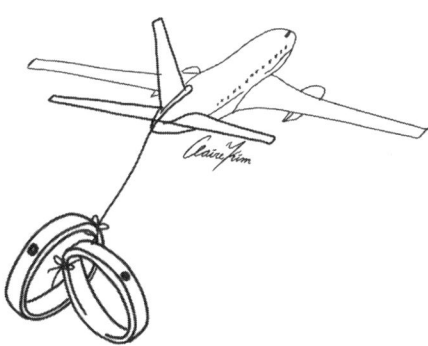

Running on Crutches

August 19, 2022

Not long ago, I came across a Facebook post by an acquaintance about Glacier National Park. It described the breathtaking scenery on the way down from Banff National Park in Canada. While I agreed with the sentiment, what suddenly came to mind was something else entirely—my younger son's crutches, which he had used all summer about 20 years ago.

At the time, he had just finished 5th grade. I had been wondering how to keep him engaged over the summer break, and eventually decided to send him to a three-week summer camp. His older brother had attended a similar camp before, so even though the younger one was still in elementary school, we chose a residential program at a college campus a couple of hours from home. That same summer, his brother was off at a different camp, so my wife and I looked forward to enjoying a few weeks of peace and quiet at home. That hope, however, was shattered the very next day.

I got a call from the camp director—calling from a hospital. His first words were, "Do not be alarmed," clearly meant to reassure me. He explained that my son had been playing soccer during free time when another student attempted a tackle but ended up kicking my son's ankle instead of the ball. It turned out to be a fracture, and he was taken to the hospital. Fortunately, the growth plate was unharmed, and after the bone was realigned, his leg was put in a cast.

When I spoke with my son directly, he did not seem to be in much pain but asked to come home due to the discomfort and limited mobility. I encouraged him to stay at least one more day, and he agreed. The next day, I drove to the camp to bring him home. But once there, he did not seem as distressed as I had imagined. Though it was clearly difficult for him to shower and get around on crutches, I suggested, "If you come home now, you will not be able to return—why not try just one more day?" He agreed.

True to my word, I returned the following day. I asked how he had managed. He said he had simply gotten around using the crutches. When I asked again whether he wanted to come home, he said yes, but his conviction was not as strong as before. So, I offered another option: "Why not stay just a few more days? I will come again over the weekend." The camp offered to move his room to the first floor to help. He decided to give it a few more days.

That weekend, I visited again, and we had a similar conversation. I said, "You can always go home—but once you do, there will be nothing much to do there. Is it not better to stay and participate in what you still can?" I framed it as both a question and a gentle persuasion. In the end, we succeeded—he completed the full three-week program.

After both boys had finished their camps, we went ahead with our previously planned family vacation. This time, we packed crutches and a wheelchair along with us. Starting in Arizona, we made our way through Salt Lake City and Yellowstone before arriving at Glacier National Park in Montana. Our final destination was Banff in Canada, just across the border. Yet surprisingly, I found Glacier National Park more appealing than Banff—it had a quieter, more peaceful charm.

After dinner one evening, we decided to take a walk through the forest trail. There were signs posted along the way: "Beware of Bears," with instructions on what to do in case of an encounter. We discussed the signs in detail as we walked. Then, all of a sudden, we looked up the path ahead—and there it was: a bear, just up the trail, turning its head to look directly at us.

We all froze.

No one needed to say a word. We all immediately turned around, just as the signs had advised. While it said not to run, our walking pace might as well have been a sprint.

And the fastest among us?

The one on crutches!

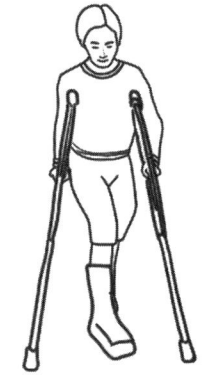

Feedback from Son

August 9, 2024

A week or two ago, I asked my younger son, who lives far away, for a favor. I was preparing to meet with ninth-grade students and their parents at church and needed a short video to show at that gathering. I planned to have all participants introduce themselves and share one or two of their strengths and weaknesses, so I thought I would go first and asked him to make a video about me. Thankfully, he did not turn me down and sent three short clips, each tailored to a different prompt. Watching them brought a flood of thoughts.

Looking back on raising my two sons, now in their thirties, I realize I rarely had a chance to hear directly how I came across to them. The only memory that stands out is from my older son's elementary school diary, where he complained about being nagged to do things even during vacation. He had just come back from a tiring Boy Scout camp, and he wrote about how contradictory it was for us to tell him to rest while also asking him to be productive. He bluntly suggested that we parents needed to change our ways. I did not give it much thought at the time, convincing myself that I was not the one nagging—his mother was. I brushed it off, thinking I was not the type to nag.

Even after the boys went off to college, we kept in touch and had ongoing conversations, sometimes with clashing views.

But having different opinions seemed natural, and I saw those serious conversations as signs of a healthy relationship. What I appreciated most was that my sons did not dismiss me as old-fashioned—they listened to me, and through them, I got glimpses into more current ways of thinking.

We shared laughter, occasional outrage, and words of encouragement. But I do not recall ever asking how they saw me. I was so used to being the one giving advice or guidance that I never thought to ask for feedback. I had not asked what they considered my strengths or weaknesses, nor had I created space for them to share that even if they wanted to.

But this time, watching the videos my younger son had made, I realized I should have opened that dialogue much earlier. While the content was mostly what I expected, it included a few things I had long forgotten. Even in a 30-second video, I was surprised to see what had stayed with him—things I had taken lightly but were memorable for him.

The video about my strengths was generally what I had anticipated. Of course, it felt good to hear those words—just like the saying "Even whales will dance when praised," I found myself smiling. But then came the 10-second clip pointing out something I needed to improve. My immediate impulse was to call him and argue back: "You are wrong," "When did I ever do that?" and so on.

Nobody enjoys being criticized—especially not by their own children. I have spent decades as a lawyer advising clients, and over 20 years as a school board member giving feedback to school district staff. Giving advice comes naturally to me.

Receiving it, not so much. Maybe it is my personality, or maybe it is a professional habit I have picked up over the years.

Though I have long passed the age Confucius called "the age when the ears are obedient" (age sixty, when one is said to listen without resistance), my ears still seem rough and unrefined. Still, after sitting with my son's comments, I am glad I resisted the urge to argue and instead sent him a message of thanks. It was difficult, but maybe this kind of feedback is something I need to hear more often.

Tomorrow, at the ninth-grade church meeting, parents will get a chance to hear from their own children. I wonder how frank the kids will be—and how the parents will take it. Some might be caught off guard or get defensive; others may accept it thoughtfully. Honestly, I am a little excited to see how it will all unfold.

What is More Important?

January 8, 2001
Radio AM 1310

Last Thursday, my older son had a choir concert. He is now in 7th grade and has chosen choir as one of his electives at school. The concert was originally scheduled before the start of winter break, but on the day of the concert, heavy snow caused the school to close, and the concert was automatically postponed.

The rescheduled date—last Thursday—happened to conflict with a meeting I had committed to long ago. I asked my son, "What should I do? I have a meeting I really need to attend." And he asked me, "Dad, what is more important—me or the meeting?" I was caught off guard for a moment. I quickly gathered myself and replied, "Of course, you are more important."

Later, I found out that this question—"What is more important?" —was something he had picked up from his younger brother, who was in 4th grade. Apparently, the younger one uses it whenever he wants to play with his older brother, and the older one tries to get out of it by saying he has homework or something else to do. He would then say, "What is more important—me or your homework?"

Fortunately, I was able to handle the meeting over the phone and make it to the concert on time. Still, the question I was asked that day left me feeling like I had been struck on the back of the head. It made me wonder whether that question—"What is more important?"—is one I should keep asking myself again and again.

Between the law practice, community organizations I am involved with, and my role on the Fairfax County Planning Commission, I have meetings nearly every evening of the week. That leaves me very little time to be with my kids. And when I think about it, there is no question more painful and piercing than "What is more important?"

I often rationalize that I am serving the community, trying to set an example as one of the few Asian Americans in public roles within the mainstream society. But from my kids' point of view, it might just feel like they rarely get to see their dad in the evening. Maybe they have grown so used to it that they no longer expect me to be around.

Children need their parents to be present more than anything else while they are growing up. That is a truth I cannot ignore, and it makes me wonder if I have been doing it wrong. I try to make up for lost time on weekends by spending time with them. That is why I rarely play golf. I go to all their soccer and basketball games. We watch movies together. We work out together.

But even with all that, can I confidently say I have done everything I should as their father? I am not so sure.

"Dad, what is more important—me or your office work? Me or your community activities? Me or your political work?"

If any of you listeners is raising young children, I encourage you to reflect on questions like these. What is more important to you—your children or your job or business? Your children or your friends? Your children or your hobbies like golf? And when you decide what is more important—do you consistently give it priority?

Compared to TV

March 9, 1998
Radio AM 1310

"I would rather have a TV at home than my dad." I still remember a pastor once mentioning this during a sermon, referring to a survey of first-grade students where over 90% gave that answer.

About two weeks ago on a Friday morning, my fourth-grade son, Joonyoung, had a special school program, so I went. About a month and a half earlier, his homeroom teacher had mentioned during a private conversation that although there would not be a formal invitation, I should definitely come to this event called "Colonial Days." It was a program where students learned about and reenacted life during America's colonial period under British rule.

That morning, unlike usual, Joonyoung asked his mom to drive him to school early instead of taking the bus. He said he needed to practice before school started. I had not told him I was coming, and I swore his mom to secrecy too. I wanted to surprise him and make him happy.

After dropping the kids off at school, I sat in the parking lot around 9:00 AM, leisurely reading the paper. As the event was scheduled to start at 9:45, I went into the school office shortly before then, signed in, and put on a visitor badge. But I could not find the event anywhere. When I asked the office staff, they told me the program was happening throughout the school and suggested I start by checking Joonyoung's classroom.

When I got to his classroom, he was not there. One of his friends came up excitedly and said, "Joonyoung is in Mrs. Black's class." The homeroom teacher, preoccupied helping students with their costumes, did not even notice my arrival. When I approached to at least say hello, the friend added, "The only ones not wearing Colonial Days costumes are Joonyoung and the teacher." My face turned red with embarrassment. I tried to laugh it off, but it stung.

As I hesitated outside the room, trying to find Mrs. Black's class, a woman came up and asked if I was Joonyoung's dad. When I said yes, she introduced herself as the orchestra teacher and asked why I had not come to the 9:15 AM concert.

"9:15?" I asked in surprise. "Wasn't it supposed to be at 9:45?"

That morning, I could not help but think how little attention I had been paying to my kids lately. Caught up in my work on the school board, I was hardly available for them. The whole family was always busy, and it hurt to think we were not showing love and care at the time they needed it most.

Later, I asked their mom about the costume. She said Joonyoung had intentionally chosen not to wear one because it would get in the way of playing in the orchestra. I felt slightly relieved, but still reflected on how little I truly knew about what my kids were doing.

That day made me rethink everything. Why was I doing this

difficult, exhausting school board work? I often say it is "for the children," but I had to ask myself again—was it really for my child? Was I even living up to that claim?

Santa's Gift

December 29, 2000
Radio AM 1310

It was just a few days ago—Christmas. Both of our boys still firmly believed in Santa Claus. Even our oldest, who would be turning 13 in just ten days, and our younger one, age 9, were absolutely convinced that Santa personally delivered their presents. Of course, they had asked questions in past years about whether "Santa Grandpa" really existed, but even this Christmas, they insisted the gifts had come from Santa —not from Mom or Dad. Watching a nearly 13-year-old still believe in Santa made it hard to tell whether he was simply innocent or just naive, but until they discover the truth on their own, they will probably keep saying that.

On Christmas Eve, our house was filled with anticipation as we waited for Santa's visit. According to legend, Santa only brings presents after midnight on December 24, so the kids were determined to stay awake until then. Since Santa has such a tight schedule flying around the world, it was impossible to predict exactly when he would show up—so all they could do was wait.

This year, our younger son wanted to try to take a picture of Santa. Both boys were determined to meet him in person this time, so they got into bed as early as 6 p.m. But instead of sleeping, they ended up passing the time with a PlayStation game.

Fortunately, by the time midnight rolled around, they were still playing. And while they were distracted, Santa made his move. By the time they stopped playing at 12:05 and came upstairs from the basement, Santa had already been and gone. He had quietly dropped off the gifts sometime between 12:00 and 12:05. Their mom, who was upstairs at the time, recalled hearing a strange sound from the first floor but did not realize that it was Santa. So once again, they failed to catch him in the act.

But Santa did not forget their gifts. Among the presents were a few books, and videotapes about Thomas Edison and Pope John Paul II. There were also a couple of bigger gifts—a microscope and a Walkman. According to mom, the younger one had mentioned wanting a microscope several times the previous year, and we had assumed the Walkman would be more fitting for our older son, who was finally becoming a teenager.

As the boys opened their gifts one by one, the microscope finally appeared. Mom and I looked forward to seeing the younger one's joyful reaction. But to our surprise, the moment he saw the microscope, he said, "This looks like something my brother would like," and handed it to him. Next came the Walkman. Upon opening it, the younger one clutched it tightly and exclaimed, "Thank you, Santa!" claiming it as his own.

At that moment, we did not know quite how to react. I could only clutch my stomach and laugh, while Mom tried to smooth things over, suggesting, "How about your brother uses the Walkman, and you keep the microscope?"

This little episode reminded us once again how wrong parents could be when they thought they knew everything about their kids. The microscope had been a wish from over a year ago, and our assumption that the Walkman would only appeal to a teenager turned out to be completely off. This Christmas taught us the importance of having more conversations with our children and paying closer attention to what they actually like.

Next year, let's hope Santa does not make the same mistake.

Parent's Growing Pains

January 25, 2013

Last weekend, I watched my younger son return to school after winter break. Now a college senior, this was his last winter vacation—just one more semester until graduation. I used to wonder when the kids would finally finish school so I could feel a little freer. But now that the moment is fast approaching, I feel a strange emptiness. The days of nagging them or paying their tuition are numbered, and oddly, I find myself feeling sentimental about that.

I have two sons. Since I never had a daughter, I cannot speak to what that relationship would be like. But looking back on life with my boys, I began to realize somewhere along the way that they no longer viewed my authority the same way they once had. I am not sure exactly when it started, but it became obvious during high school—especially with the younger one, who may have begun tuning me out much earlier. The older one seemed more obedient, at least on the surface, but perhaps he felt the same way deep down. Yet, until they graduated high school and lived at home, they at least pretended to listen. Everything changed once they entered college.

I imagine my kids eagerly looked forward to leaving home—what could be more exciting than tasting freedom without parental interference? But as they headed off to school, I suddenly lost touch with their daily lives and inner thoughts. With fewer ways to help, I started to question my role as a father. Should I step back and simply observe? Or should I still occasionally speak up? I did not know what the right balance was.

When my older son reached his senior year and began thinking about life after graduation, I realized I had very little useful advice to offer. He had more current knowledge about job markets and graduate school options than I did. What direction could I possibly give him? That moment brought into sharp focus how powerless I was becoming in this role. And I could only imagine that this sense of limitation would grow stronger in the years ahead.

My younger son told me he wanted to go to graduate school. He talked about his desired field of study and the schools he planned to apply to, but I did not know anything about that area. All I could do was listen. His list of schools did not include any of the "elite" institutions I had in mind. I realized then that I was slowly being distanced from their choices and decisions. My parents probably felt the same way about me when I was younger. I recall resisting their advice when they tried to comment on my career path. Now the roles have reversed.

When my younger son was about to return to school after break, I asked if he would stay a few more days. I figured it might be better to rest at home since his dorm's dining hall likely was not open yet. But his response caught me off guard: "I can only really rest once I am back at school."

Home was no longer his sanctuary. The dorm had become his

safe and familiar space. Our house was no longer "home," but rather "my parents' place"—a stopover during school breaks. He likely no longer saw it as coming home, but as visiting us.

I did not know how to respond to that. But it reminded me of how I had felt returning home during college. Probably starting in my sophomore year, while it was always comforting to come back to my parents' house, it never truly felt like where I belonged anymore. Being at school felt more like "my place," and home sometimes felt like a retreat or escape. Now my sons feel the same way.

Although neither of my children lives with me now, both the college graduate and the one preparing for graduate school are no longer "kids under my care." I know it is only natural that they should be free to fly on their own—but emotionally, I have not fully caught up to that reality. Perhaps this is what it means to grow and mature as a parent.

Conditions for Marriage

April 19, 2024

Last November, after wrapping up the Fairfax County School Board election, I visited Korea and made a stop in Taiwan, where I formally met my daughter-in-law's parents for the first time.

Due to the pandemic, they were unable to attend their daughter's wedding held in the U.S., so this trip served as our first official meeting. Strictly speaking, it was not the first time we had crossed paths. My son and his wife were college classmates who graduated the same year. Back in the spring of 2010, I had briefly met my daughter-in-law's parents when they came for the graduation ceremony. But my son and his wife were just friends at the time, so the encounter amounted to a brief greeting. That means our proper meeting came after thirteen and a half years.

My daughter-in-law's parents are Taiwanese. They had studied in the U.S., completed their degrees, and worked professionally here before their daughter was born.[20] As such, she is an American-born U.S. citizen. But during her childhood, the family decided to return to Taiwan, where she attended school

---

20) My older son's mother-in-law earned her master's degree from Boston University, and his father-in-law received his Ph.D. from Harvard University. His father-in-law, Moo Woong Lim (林茂雄), is a researcher, inventor, and entrepreneur. He has now significantly scaled back his activities.

through high school. She then came back to the U.S. for college, where she met my son. After years of dating, breaking up, and eventually navigating a long-distance relationship, they got married.

I never told my son that he had to marry another Korean. I simply said that as long as the person was a Christian and someone he loved, that was enough. So, when he introduced his Taiwanese girlfriend and said they planned to marry, I congratulated them without hesitation. During our first formal meeting, I made no special demands. I simply thanked her for loving our son and asked what she liked about him.

Later, my son told me he planned to call her parents to formally ask for their blessing. But a few days after, I learned that they had requested he come to Taiwan to do it in person. It was a long journey and not an easy time for travel, but he had no choice—so he went.

After that trip, I asked my son how it went. He said nothing unusual had happened. But this past fall, when I met my in-laws in Taiwan, I learned about that meeting from an entirely different perspective.

"If a daughter brings a boyfriend all the way to Taiwan to introduce him to her parents, the decision to marry has already been made. There is little the parents can say at that point."

When I heard that, I realized they may have initially had some reservations about my son—perhaps, in part, because he was not Taiwanese.

However, rather than oppose the marriage, they had set some

conditions. And when I heard what those conditions were, I could not help but admire their wisdom. They were unique, realistic, and ultimately beneficial to my son.

The first was weight loss. Ah—this was something I had long wanted to bring up myself, and it was as if they had read my mind.

The second was to pursue further education. Again, that was exactly what I had hoped for. At the time, my son only held a bachelor's degree, while his girlfriend had already earned her doctorate.

The final condition was to learn Chinese. I wholeheartedly agreed. I had taken a year off college myself to study Chinese in Taiwan, so I knew its importance firsthand. Just as I hoped my daughter-in-law would one day learn some Korean, it made perfect sense for my son to study Chinese.

To my in-laws, I want to say thank you again—for presenting these three thoughtful, doable, and meaningful conditions.

My daughter-in-law's father: he and my daughter-in-law look like two peas in a pod.

Signing his own book, 'Moore's Journey.' Part of the copy of my book *Hamburger Coke* that I signed and gave him is visible.

Chapter 7
Food Stories

Introduction

There is a question often asked: "Do we live to eat, or eat to live?" The correct answer may vary depending on one's perspective, but one undeniable truth that emerges from this question is the significance of eating itself. Eating is not merely about supplying the body with necessary nutrients. The food we eat reflects our very way of life. Our culture, taste preferences, needs, daily routines, and surroundings all influence what we eat.

In the days when we lived in poverty in Korea, there were few food choices. Eating three meals a day was a struggle, and the reason we were almost forced to eat mixed grains for lunch was not for health, but because of a shortage of rice. Meat was a rare luxury, only enjoyed on special occasions. We had no snacks, and imported foods were beyond our dreams.

But when we came to America, food suddenly became abundant. Although we continued eating mainly Korean food at home, I was exposed to many unfamiliar foods for the first time—bananas, pineapples, hot dogs, pizza, and spaghetti, to name a few. When I was in high school, my mother would occasionally try making hamburgers, but she used so much onion and garlic that I had to open the classroom windows during lunch to air out the smell.

In my freshman year of college, I once mistook yogurt in the cafeteria for a dip for potato chips. Before coming to the U.S., my only exposure to Chinese food was the cheap Korean-style noodle dishes or sweet-and-sour pork on very rare few occasions. So, when I was invited by a friend's family to an American-style Chinese restaurant during the freshman orientation week in college and was served Moo Shu pork as an appetizer, I had no idea how to eat it. I ended up awkwardly tearing the accompanying pancakes with my hands—a moment that I remember breaking into a nervous sweat.[21]

While not all of the foods in this chapter were new to me when I arrived in America, the stories behind them hold precious memories.

---

21) The story of Moo Shu Pork was included in my 2020 book *Sky Castle School Board Member Stories* (*Hamburger Coke*, English edition).

Acorn Jello

May 8, 2020

In Korea, May 8 is celebrated as Parents' Day. Before I immigrated to the United States, it used to be called "Mother's Day," but the name was changed to "Parents' Day" in 1973. In the U.S., Mother's Day is observed on the second Sunday of May each year, which this year falls on May 10. Father's Day is on the third Sunday in June.

It has been quite a while since my mother passed away. I have tried not to dwell on memories of her, who left this world too early. The regret of not having done more for her in life was too painful, and I did not trust myself to manage emotions. So, I avoided thinking about her.

Like most grandmothers, my mother adored her grandchildren. Though my two younger sisters also had children, they lived out of state, so my mother poured all her love into the two grandchildren who lived nearby—my sons. After I got married and moved out, my mother helped care for our children when they were young. We thought it was better than leaving them with someone else, and my mother seemed happy to do it. I am sure it was not easy, but she never once complained.

At first, a misunderstanding led to a difficult moment. We gave her some money for helping with the kids—thinking of it as pocket money—but she was hurt by the gesture. I told her we knew she was not watching the kids for pay, but her feelings were not easily soothed. Eventually, we started giving her money to spend on whatever she wanted to buy for the grandkids, and that gradually helped ease the tension.

Originally, my parents lived in Alexandria, Virginia. But to be closer to their grandchildren, they moved to Fairfax. My father, who was still working at the time, had to commute to Washington, D.C., which made things less convenient, but he accepted the trouble for the sake of the grandchildren.

At my mother's memorial service, my younger son gave a tribute. He was already in college but still affectionately called "my puppy" by his grandmother. It was then that I heard many of the stories for the first time. I was reminded once again of the deep love she had for her grandchildren.

In front of our house are oak trees. In the fall, acorns would ripen and drop, and my mother would collect them to make acorn jello (dotorimuk). Watching her compete with squirrels for the acorns was amusing, but seeing those acorns transformed into a side dish or snack was even more fascinating.

Once, when my younger son went on a school field trip in elementary school, he found himself in a place with many oak trees. Seeing all the acorns on the ground, he immediately thought of his grandmother. Wanting to please her, he carefully picked only the biggest and best-looking acorns and brought them home with pride.

After getting off the school bus at his grandmother's house, he ran inside and proudly presented the acorns he had gathered. As expected, his grandmother was delighted. But then something unexpected happened—most of the beautiful-looking acorns were filled with worms. More than disappointment, my son felt sorry toward his grandmother. But she did not say a word. Instead, she calmly took out a knife, gently cut away the worm-eaten parts, and gathered the good portions to make acorn jello.

That memory, of his grandmother wrapping her grandchild's heartfelt gesture with grandmotherly love, deeply moved me during her memorial service. That is how she lived her entire life.

Now, watching my two sons who are grown, and remembering this story as Mother's Day approaches, I find myself wondering whether I have offered them the same kind of love. But I cannot answer that question with confidence.

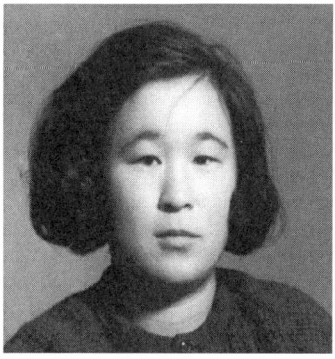

A photo of my mother (my children's grandmother) in her twenties.

A photo of the children with their grandmother and grandfather, taken in June 1995 after I was sworn in for the first time as an appointed school board member.

In front of Grandma's house.

Popcorn

May 1, 2020

I love popcorn. Rather than buying pre-popped popcorn, I prefer to get dried corn kernels and pop them myself at home. I put a bit of oil in a frying pan or Chinese-style wok, add a handful of kernels, cover it with a lid, and heat it up. As the kernels gradually warm up, you start to hear the popping sound. When the popping gets louder and then starts to taper off, it means the popcorn is ready.

There is a funny story involving popcorn. It happened when my younger son was in high school. At the time, he was on the school basketball team. It was a science magnet high school, so the team was not exactly a powerhouse, but the players were passionate, and their dedication was second to none. The parents supporting the team were equally devoted.

High school basketball teams in Fairfax County are divided into three levels: the Varsity team, the Junior Varsity (JV) team, and the Freshman team, which consists solely of ninth graders. Usually, all three teams play on the same day—starting with the Freshman game, followed by the JV game, and ending with the Varsity game.

When there was a home game, many volunteers were needed. Some sold tickets at the box office, others checked tickets and handed out programs at the entrance, and some operated the game clock during the Freshman and JV games. Among all these roles, the biggest responsibility was running the snack bar. While gate revenue was shared between the two schools playing, all snack bar profits went to the home team. That is why the parents took turns volunteering. You could watch your own child's game, but during the others, you had to help out.

During the four years my son played basketball, I volunteered many times. Of all the roles, I found working the snack bar the most fun—and the most technical. You had to actually prepare simple food items, and popcorn was one of them. But making popcorn at a game was nothing like doing it at home. You had to produce much larger quantities and use a popcorn machine. I had to learn how to operate the machine, and it was not easy for someone like me who was not used to it.

One day, my wife and I were in charge of the snack bar by ourselves. While making popcorn for the halftime crowd, I burned a batch due to my carelessness. Smoke started to fill the snack bar, but the ventilation was not adequate. Soon the smoke alarm went off. Since the alarm was connected to the gym, the game had to be stopped, and all the players and spectators had to evacuate the building according to safety protocols.

Soon, a fire truck arrived. Once the firefighters confirmed there was no real danger, the game was allowed to resume. And by that point, the cause of the smoke had been identified. Though many people offered me words of comfort, I was still incredibly embarrassed.

But that was not the end of it.

After the game resumed, I cleaned up the burnt popcorn and

tried again—only to burn another batch. Again, the game was stopped, and again the fire truck was dispatched. I had managed to interrupt the same game twice—an unprecedented incident. That night, I became known both as the guy who stopped the game and as the dad who happened to be a school board member.

Afterward, some parents jokingly lobbied me, saying that since I was on the school board, maybe I could secure some funding to improve the school's ventilation system.

Among all the volunteer experiences I have had as a parent, that day remains one of the most unforgettable.

Cold Water

May 22, 1998
The Washington Media

"Dad, why do you drink beer?"

"Well, when I am especially thirsty, it feels really refreshing."

"You could just drink cold water."

"You are right… but beer helps me relax and eases the fatigue a little."

"That is what they say about drugs, too."

"……."

This happened about three or four weeks ago. As usual, I had returned home late at night after attending a meeting related to the school board. That night, I was particularly thirsty and tired. I vaguely remembered there being a bottle of beer left in the fridge, so I went to look for it. When I could not find it, I rushed upstairs and asked my wife if we had any left—only to be met with the above challenge from my older son, a fourth grader.

As the conversation with my son unfolded, I felt a jolt of realization. I had nothing convincing left to say. My explanation lacked weight and clearly was not educational—it even seemed like a shortcut to losing authority and respect as a father. In the end, I gave up on finding that beer.

Raising two elementary school boys, I constantly try to be a role model, but there are countless moments when I catch myself being contradictory. I am sure that I am not the only one. Take, for example, driving on the highway. The posted speed limit is clearly fifty-five miles per hour—but how many parents actually follow that? Don't many people, with their children in the car, go ten miles over the limit, justifying it by thinking it is okay as long as the police are not around? Does breaking the law become acceptable if you are not caught? Or is speeding just not considered a real violation anymore? Is it okay to ignore traffic laws?

At school, students are taught that smoking and drinking—just like drugs—are harmful. They emphasize that tobacco, in particular, is highly addictive and should never be used. But are there not parents who still smoke in front of their children?

Not long ago, I had the opportunity to review a video that all Fairfax County 6th graders are required to watch as part of the "Family Life Education" curriculum. The video emphasized that tobacco-related deaths far outnumber those from drugs or drunk driving. It explained how smoking is a financial drain and a danger to those around the smoker. If adults downplay the seriousness of smoking, what message will children get when comparing school lessons with their parents' behavior? What will they learn? What will they think of their parents?

Are there parents out there who give alcohol to their underage children under the logic that "they should learn to drink from their parents?" Some argue that low-alcohol beverages like beer or wine are okay. While adults drinking is not necessarily wrong, what matters most is instilling values and character that children can emulate.

I, too, occasionally have a glass of beer or wine, or offer it to guests. But I remind myself that every action we take can influence our children. If our words and deeds do not align, we risk raising children who see hypocrisy as normal.

Let us not forget the importance of being mindful in everything we do—because our children are always watching.

Pizza and Bagels

April 24, 2020

Until I immigrated to the United States in 1974, during my high school years, I had never heard of pizza or bagels. I did not know what they looked like—let alone what they tasted like. Before entering college, the only pizzas I had ever had were frozen pizzas from the grocery store that we baked in the oven at home and one time at Pizza Hut with my high school classmates. As for bagels, I had never even tried one.

But once I started college, pizza became a more regular part of my life. It was especially tempting late at night when I was studying in my dorm room and wanted a break under the pretense of needing to satisfy my hunger. After supper in the dorm dining room, I usually got back to my room before 7 p.m. I would sit down to study, but by around 10 p.m., it became difficult to concentrate. It felt too early to stop or go to bed, but the work piled up and I could not simply quit. That is when hunger became a convenient excuse. And, somehow, I always got hungry around that time.

There was a pizza place near the dorm that a close friend and I frequented. The place was always packed with students at that time. Sometimes we had to wait for a seat, but more often than not, we could sit down and order right away. Our usual was pepperoni pizza—greasy, probably the unhealthiest topping, but also the most irresistible.

The only real dilemma was the size. Since we had come out to grab a quick bite before getting back to studying, having just one or two slices seemed ideal. But inevitably, my friend and I would agree that a medium-size pizza was the minimum. And for just two dollars more, we could get a large, which was double the size. It seemed like the more "economical" choice. So, we would order the large—and finish every last slice.

Afterward came the guilt. But it was comforting to know I was not the only one—my friend was in it with me.

Unfortunately, that was not the end of it.

Trying to go back to studying on a full stomach was not easy. I felt too bloated to sit still. So, we would drop by the snack corner on the first floor of the dorm to play a round of foosball. You could play one-on-one, but it was more fun with teams of two. My friend and I would team up against other students. If you won, you stayed on the table. If you lost, you waited your turn to play again. We would get so into the game that not only did we digest the food, but we would sometimes get hungry again—and then order bagels from the snack bar.

I was introduced to bagels for the first time in college. But late at night, nothing beat a toasted bagel with cream cheese. It was so good, I would even jokingly beg for a little extra cream cheese.

After bagels and more rounds of foosball, time would fly. It would be way past bedtime by the time I returned to my room. There was no energy left to study. In just a few hours, I would have to wake up, wash, eat breakfast, and head to class.

That cycle repeated itself throughout my college years. The stress of studying was met with illogical and unhealthy coping habits. Looking at my round belly today, I would not be surprised if much of the fat dates back to those college days.

I recently heard that the pizza place we used to visit so often is no longer there. I am not sure when it closed, but it is gone now. That is disappointing—not just because of the taste, but because the place held so many memories shared with a good friend. The pizza we had there was not just food—it was part of our college experience and remains an unforgettable taste to this day.

Egg Foo Young

May 22, 2020

One of the changes brought on by the COVID-19 pandemic these days is an increase in home cooking. Even people who previously had little interest in cooking are now boldly giving it a try. On Facebook, you often see photos of home-cooked dishes, and even husbands who used to rely entirely on their wives in the kitchen are proudly showing off their culinary creations—delighting viewers and stimulating both appetite and curiosity.

I have never been one for cooking, but recently, I tried something that I hardly dare call "cooking"—making a rolled omelet. Since it was my first attempt, I naturally had to start by searching for a recipe. I watched a few YouTube videos and chose the simplest method. Still, I learned a couple of things in the process: you need to start rolling the omelet when it is about 70% cooked, and you should not pour all the egg mixture into the pan at once. Instead, you pour in about half to start, then roll it and add the rest in two portions as space becomes available in the pan.

My first-ever rolled omelet turned out better than expected, which made me ambitious. This time, I decided to add more of the vegetables I like. Ignoring the recipe, I chopped up a generous amount of vegetables and mixed them into the eggs. The result looked more like the batter for Korean mung bean pancakes (bindaetteok) that my mother used to make. As you might expect, it did not roll up neatly—parts burst open here and there, and it ended up more like an American-style vegetable omelet.

That is when I was suddenly reminded of Egg Foo Young, a dish I used to enjoy during my college days.

Back in college, I often headed to the MIT campus on weekends. Although I attended Harvard, I had more close friends at MIT. There were some Korean students like me at MIT who had immigrated to the U.S. relatively late, but most of the Korean students at Harvard had either been born in the U.S. or had immigrated at a young age. Because I had only been in the country for a few years, I found it difficult to fit in—both with Americans and with Korean students who had grown up in the U.S.

With my MIT friends, Friday evenings often meant dinner in Boston's Chinatown. Chinatown back then was not very large, but for us college students, it was a place where we could get a hearty meal at a reasonable price. And our go-to dish was Egg Foo Young. This Chinese-style omelet was affordable and filling. You could pay a little extra to add meat or seafood, but since we were always short on cash, we usually stuck with the basic version filled with vegetables. I remember it had a lot of onions. The egg mixture was pan-fried, placed over a bed of rice, and topped generously with hot gravy. Served in a big bowl, it was the perfect way to cap off a tough week and share a meal with friends.

After dinner, we had a tradition: watching three back-to-back Chinese films at a nearby movie theater. They were usually martial arts or romance films, and this triple feature was the most entertainment we could afford as students. Once we entered the dark theater, at first, we could not see who else was there, but as time went on, we began recognizing familiar faces. Often, we would spot older doctoral students. As they had no girlfriends and only little money, they spent their weekends just like we undergraduates did—in Chinatown, watching movies and escaping the pressures of school.

When we spotted them, we felt obligated to go over and say hello, though they always looked a bit awkward. Looking back now, I fondly picture their bashful smiles to be endearing. Many of those seniors went on to return to Korea and hold high-ranking positions, but back then, they were just ordinary international students, eating Egg Foo Young in humble Chinatown diners and worrying about their studies and future.

The restaurants and theaters we used to frequent are gone now. But in my heart, they remain vividly alive. Though I can no longer visit them in person, they are places I can always return to in my memory.

Ramen

April 17, 2020

Today, I would like to talk a bit about ramen.

At one point during the COVID-19 pandemic, ramen became one of the most stockpiled items among Korean Americans. It is inexpensive, easy to cook, and commonly enjoyed not just as a snack but also as a full meal. In the past, there were only a few varieties, but now there are so many that I cannot even remember all their names.

I have not eaten ramen for quite some time. It tastes great, but I have heard it is not the healthiest food, so I try to avoid it. My father's case, however, is a different story. He immigrated to the U.S. a year before our family did, in 1973, and he is what you would call a ramen enthusiast—although even that word does not quite capture it. Ever since coming to the U.S., he has eaten ramen every morning for breakfast.

He usually just adds one or two eggs or a few slices of rice cake—hardly any other ingredients. Sometimes he even eats it for lunch, too. No matter how much I try to tell him it is not good for his health, it does not work.

"I am 87 years old, and I have been eating ramen every day for 50 years. Does that not show that it is not that bad?"

I could not argue with that logic. Still, knowing he has high blood pressure, I tried to persuade him to cut down on sodium.

He insisted that ramen does not contain that much sodium, so we looked at the nutrition label on the packaging together.

The ramen he enjoys had over 40% of the recommended daily sodium intake—per serving. He looked at the number and calmly said, "Then I will just stay under 60% for the rest of the day."

But when I explained that each packet was two servings, he looked genuinely surprised. He had never imagined that one packet was meant to be for two people. Yet, he did not give up ramen. Instead, he started using only half or a third of the seasoning packet. At first, he said it was too bland, but over time, he got used to it. Now he says it tastes too salty if he uses the whole packet.

I am also reminded of my freshman year of college.

I used to bring ramen from home in Virginia to eat when I got hungry while studying late at night. Cooking and eating ramen in the dorm room was a real treat. At first, my three white roommates just stared at me curiously. But after tasting a few strands, they started offering to pay me to cook them a packet each.

Looking back, I should have charged them more.

But I only calculated the cost, which came out to be about twenty-five cents per pack. Since it was so cheap, they ordered without hesitation, and before I knew it, all the ramen I had brought to savor was gone. I could not raise the price, and I could not refuse the purchase orders, either. It was an awkward situation.

That experience taught me that sharing ramen is not always easy—but even I once imposed on someone else for ramen.

It was during law school.

There were quite a few Korean undergraduates at the time, and I was considered an older sibling ("hyung" or "oppa") figure to them. One of the younger students lived in the dorm but rarely ate in the dining hall. He preferred cooking for himself or buying food from outside. I would often crash in his room, and his staple food was ramen.

Ramen was perfect for time-strapped students because it was quick and easy to make. But most importantly, it was cheap. For a student with limited financial resources, it was a practical choice. The problem was that whenever he started cooking ramen late at night, other Korean students would start showing up one by one. And before long, the full box of ramen he kept would be gone.

Even I, the older student, shamelessly joined in. Looking back, it is quite embarrassing. I should have brought a few boxes of ramen myself to share. Instead, I just kept mooching.

Every time I see that student—now an adult—I remember how sorry I felt. I still feel like I owe him boxes of ramen.

The person seated on the left playing the guitar is Pastor Sun-Wook Chang, who frequently generously gifted (?) me a large supply of ramen. He came up with a friend to share music at my victory celebration after the 2023 school board election.

Ice Cream

May 26, 2023

Suddenly, I craved ice cream.

It was last Saturday, the day of in-person caucus voting for the Democratic endorsement for the Fairfax County School Board election. In-person voting took place for just one day, from 10 a.m. to 4 p.m., and online voting, which had been ongoing for a week, was also scheduled to end at the same time.

Perhaps due to several nights of restless sleep, I woke up very early that morning. Still groggy, I reached for a cup of coffee. Thankfully, a student volunteer who had previously needed a ride texted to say that he did not need one after all. That gave me a bit of extra time.

I debated what to have for breakfast and settled on something warm. I fried three eggs. Biting into a yolk that was still slightly runny gave me an odd sense of comfort. I felt full and ready. I packed a simple lunch: two bananas, one orange, a hard-boiled egg, a steamed sweet potato, and two bottles of water. Once everything was ready, I headed to the polling station expected to have the most voters.

The weather was clear and sunny. By the end of the day, the Democratic endorsees for the Fairfax County School Board would be decided. Out of over 1,000 registered Democrats and 3,300 general voters, fewer than 150 were required to vote in person. Still, some would likely show up at the polling place, so I could not afford to take any vote for granted. I had to leave a good impression on anyone who came.

Around 11 a.m., I received a call from the coordinator of a senior voter group. They asked if it would be possible to send a car an hour earlier than scheduled. I contacted the volunteer drivers, and fortunately, they said it was doable. Whew...

But even after a couple of hours, the number of voters arriving at the site could be counted on one hand. Around noon, a student volunteer arrived, but with such a low turnout, the atmosphere felt awkwardly quiet. I felt almost guilty about taking out all the lunch I had brought, so I quickly ate just one banana to ease my hunger.

With me at the polling site there were another at-large candidate and the candidate for the Hunter Mill district. The three of us stood around chatting to pass the time. Whenever a voter did appear, we all rushed to greet him with enthusiastic politeness. The results were scheduled to be announced around 4:30 p.m., likely via text message to the candidates.

With 30 minutes left before polls closed, hunger hit me again. I shoved the boiled egg into my mouth—my fourth egg of the day.

Then 4 p.m. arrived.

Only thirteen voters had come to that polling station.

As soon as voting ended, I quickly gathered the flyers and lunchboxes we had prepared for voters. I paused briefly, wondering where to go next. Then, ice cream popped into my mind. I needed something sweet. Days of poor sleep and the long hours spent standing outside the polling site had taken their toll. I felt completely drained.

I drove straight to a convenience store and bought an ice cream cone. I devoured it in an instant. Only then did I start to feel somewhat humanlike again.

4:20 p.m. It was almost time for the results. Where should I go? Home? No—I needed to go to the Democratic Party headquarters. I kept checking my phone as I drove. Whenever the screen went dark, I turned it back on immediately. It was almost 4:30, but still no message.

Anxious, I messaged one of the candidates I was friendly with.

"Any news yet?"

"Nothing."

Relief. At least it did not mean that I had lost.

4:30 p.m. Still no message. I kept checking my screen as I drove. Then, at 4:37 p.m., a message came in—from the chair of the school board. My heart pounded as I clicked on it.

Just one word:

"Congratulations!"

My father passed away this past January.

Suddenly, I craved my father.

Closing Notes

As I neared the completion of preparing the Korean version of my second book, Skyhill School Board Member Stories, I found myself just days away from attending the funeral of Congressman Gerry Connolly, someone I had known for many years. Congressman Connolly and I first ran for office together in 1995—he as a candidate for County Supervisor, and I as a candidate for the School Board. We were both elected. He later became Chairman of the Board of Supervisors and, beginning in 2009, went on to serve in the U.S. House of Representatives, winning nine consecutive terms. Sadly, he passed away in May of this year while undergoing treatment after his cancer returned.

This year, I have had to say goodbye not only to Congressman Connolly, but also to two other friends who, like me, were elected to the School Board for the first time 30 years ago. In February, Bob Frye—the first black Chair of the School Board—passed away. Then, in April, Janie Strauss, who served as a School Board member for 26 years, also passed. They were all older than I, but Congressman Connolly was only 75—just seven years my senior.

Their passing has made me reflect deeply. It has led me to consider how best to spend the time I have left in my life. As I selected, reread, and edited the essays for this book, I found myself wondering what kinds of writings I might include if I ever publish another book someday. One realization I have come to while working on this second book is that I have fewer ambitions this time than I did with my first. On the other hand, I feel a lingering unease—wondering whether the content is worth sharing with readers, and questioning myself for having prepared this book at all. I sometimes worry whether I may have been caught up in self-indulgence. Perhaps adding this closing note is, in some unconscious way, a plea for the reader's generosity and a shield against criticism.

But at this point, it is too late to halt publication. I also cannot disappoint Claire Kim, a high school student who graciously collaborated with me even amid her busy life. Perhaps I chose a high school partner in the first place so I would be less likely to give up halfway through. Thanks to her, I found myself working furiously so that she could refer to this book in her college application essays.

At an event with Mr. Bob Frye

With Janie Strauss (2019)

With the late Congressman Gerry Connolly (2008)

Author and Illustrator

Claire Y. Kim, illustrator, holding the first copy of the Korean edition of this book, signed by the author on July 20, 2025.

Illustrator's Notes

Working on 'Skyhill School Board Member Stories' as an illustrator has been one of the most meaningful experiences of my life. As I read the author's writing, which chronicles his journey as a Korean immigrant, I found myself reflecting on my own family's story. His experiences were not his alone. They represent the quiet strength carried by countless immigrant families. His narrative reminded me that although immigration might be a journey marked by difficulty and uncertainty, it is also one of courage, purpose, and deep beauty. I believe every moment holds its own value, and within those moments lie endless reasons to be grateful.

As I illustrated each page, I naturally recalled cherished memories with those around me. I recently lost my former sports coach in the Flight 5342 crash, a close friend to a tragic car accident, and a former U.S. Representative from Virginia's congressional district, whom I had the honor of personally meeting through the Congressional Art Competition. In remembering them, I reflected on their absences as well as the stories we shared, the moments that shaped us, and the lasting perspectives they left with me. This project gave me an unexpected and meaningful opportunity to confront those emotions and memories.

Art has the power to communicate without words. To me, the true beauty of art lies not in its color or technique, but in its ability to create a connection between the work and its audience.

Illustration, for me, was not simply about drawing. It was a process of honoring and understanding someone else's story, and in doing so, discovering my own. I am deeply grateful to have contributed to a project that reminds us of how much there is in this world to see, to feel, and to remember.

Above all, I extend my sincere gratitude to the author for giving me the opportunity to be part of this meaningful endeavor. This project has allowed me to grow not only as an artist, but also as a person.

I hope that readers of this book find within its pages a renewed sense of courage, hope, and moments of joy in their everyday lives.

June 2025
Claire Y. Kim

Last year's Christmas family photo

Author's Other Publications

Sky Castle School Board Member Stories

Published in 2020, this book is a collection of essays by a lawyer-turned-public servant who immigrated to the U.S. with his family during high school years. Drawing from years of service as an elected school board member, the author reflects on his experiences navigating American society and civic life as a Korean immigrant. The book features a curated selection of essays from the approximately seven hundred columns he contributed to Korean American media over two decades. It offers insights not only into education but also into broader issues facing American and immigrant communities. A recommended read for parents and anyone interested in education.

Hamburger Coke

This book, published in 2021, is the English edition of Sky Castle School Board Member Stories. Its title comes from a speech the author gave at a graduation ceremony for school custodians, where he encouraged immigrant workers not to be intimidated and to confidently pursue their dreams. Through personal anecdotes and reflections, the book brings to life the immigrant experience and the realities of public education in America.

Skyhill School Board Member Stories

This is the Korean version of this book published in July 2025.